A Sense of Belonging

A Sense of Belonging

Being Church in Pluralistic Society

HILTON SCOTT

RESOURCE *Publications* • Eugene, Oregon

A SENSE OF BELONGING
Being Church in a Pluralistic Society

Copyright © 2022 Hilton Scott. All rights reserved. Except for brief quotations in critical publications or reviews, no part of this book may be reproduced in any manner without prior written permission from the publisher. Write: Permissions, Wipf and Stock Publishers, 199 W. 8th Ave., Suite 3, Eugene, OR 97401.

Resource Publications
An Imprint of Wipf and Stock Publishers
199 W. 8th Ave., Suite 3
Eugene, OR 97401

www.wipfandstock.com

PAPERBACK ISBN: 978-1-6667-3746-2
HARDCOVER ISBN: 978-1-6667-9693-3
EBOOK ISBN: 978-1-6667-9694-0

JANUARY 31, 2022 3:32 PM

Contents

List of Tables | *vi*

Acknowledgements | *vii*

Introduction | 1

Chapter 1 Key Concepts | 14

Chapter 2 Churches in Plurality | 35

Chapter 3 Interpreting the Tale: Why is This Happening? | 105

Chapter 4 Learning from Good Practice | 138

Chapter 5 A Sense of Belonging | 155

Bibliography | *169*

List of Tables

Table 1: Use of the word 'pray' in different translations of the Bible
Table 2: Modes of prayer and the threefold pattern

Acknowledgements

THIS BOOK PUBLICATION is the result of a PhD thesis written in the Faculty of Theology and Religion, University of Pretoria, South Africa.

To protect the identities of the churches and people involved, all names have been replaced with pseudonyms.

Introduction

As we pray, so we believe, so we worship—together. This is an often used translation for the aphorism: *lex orandi, lex credendi, lex (con)vivendi*. A more direct translation would be 'As we pray, so we believe, so we live (together)'.[1] The presupposition is that there are causal interrelationships between prayer (or worship), belief and being church. Consider the following as an explanation of the causal interrelatedness: as people pray (*lex orandi*), so should they believe (*lex credendi*), think and talk and as they believe think and talk, so should they live—each and everyone, together (*lex (con)vivendi*). Writing about the subject Smit contests that in a similar regard: as people live together and with one another, so should they believe, think and talk and as they believe think and talk, so should they pray. Thus, prayer affects belief, which affects being church; while belief affects prayer and being church; furthermore while being church affects prayer and belief. It is for this reason that the term 'interrelationship' is used, to accentuate the to and fro between *lex orandi*, *lex credendi*, and *lex (con)vivendi*.

By simultaneously examining prayer, what is or should be believed through prayer, and considering the appropriate aspects of being church an investigation with the purpose of liturgical inculturation was conducted. Being church in a pluralistic setting influences belief and prayer, while prayer simultaneously influences belief and being church. Such is the complex notion of *lex orandi*, *lex credendi*, and *lex (con)vivendi*. The intention of investigating prayer, belief, and being church was to better understand (1) what is going on, (2) why is this going on, (3) what ought to be going on, and (4) how might we respond.[2] Each of these questions is associated with one of each of Osmer's four core tasks for practical theological interpretation.

---

1. Smit, *Lex orandi, lex credendi, lex (con)vivendi?*, 887–907.
2. Osmer, *Practical Theology*, 4.

In response to the above statements a research problem was identified and thus a question was posed: how does the form and content of prayer impact the ways in which people connect with God and other people? The context and explanations of the research problem are engaged with as a precursor to detailing the aims associated with the research problem.

If one were to ask the question: "Who is God?" to a hundred different people, one could expect a hundred different answers which is the basic discourse of hermeneutics.[3] The notion of consumerism plays a potentially influential role in such a theory, especially regarding all too familiar questions such as: "What's in it for me?" or "What can I get out of it?." The nature of consumerism is that the self more often than not eclipses the community, the worshipper as an individual often seats him-/herself before the congregation. The popular saying goes: "The true measure of a man [or woman] is how he [or she] treats someone who can do him [or her] absolutely no good." Similarly, what a person believes is noticeable by the way in which he/she communicates with God and his/her fellow worshippers as his/her communication (*lex orandi*) should be as a result of his/her beliefs (*lex credendi*) and the way in he/she lives (*lex vivendi*).

To communicate is far more complex than simply the way a person speaks and/or listens to another. Communication also involves the language used; the emotions behind the words; the manner in which a person addresses another; the topics that are discussed; the questions that are asked and the requests that are made. Noticeable are aspects such as respect, love, honour and humility as well as the opposites: disrespect, anger, shame, and pride. Communication need not be limited to verbal forms either, there are also the abilities to communicate with body language, bodily gestures, clothing—including the style, color, and graphical displays that include written word.[4]

A metadiscourse exists between dictionary definitions and conceptual and/or contextual definitions. The term 'communicate' is not exempt from such discourse. From a sociological perspective there is not a set definition for 'communication'. However, there are different definitions that allude to simple contextual definitions. Littlejohn and Foss describe three dimensions to this differentiation. Firstly, "observation, or abstractness" where some definitions are inclusive while others are restrictive.[5] Definitions of

---

3. Schuster, *Hermeneutics As Embodied Existence*, 195–206.
4. Wepener, *The Object and Aim of Multi-Disciplinary Liturgical Research*, 384–97.
5. Littlejohn and Foss, *Theories of Human Communication*.

communication can be restrictive, for example, when sending military messages, orders and so on by telephone, telegraph, radio or courier. In this context dictionary definitions that describe a simple exchange of information are also restrictive. Secondly, there is the dimension of "intentionality" with some definitions including an intended send and receive attitude, while others are not as limiting being that there is no direct intent. Thirdly, there is the dimension of "normative judgement" which alludes to those definitions that include a statement of accuracy, success or effectiveness. These definitions typically vary from those which describe that information was shared or exchanged, to those that do not include an outcome—something was sent however not necessarily understood or received. The term 'understood' highlights a contextual element to the word 'communicate' or 'communication' because a person understands something from a certain context that is influenced by such factors as one's culture. Therefore, definitions of these words can be provided from dictionaries but importantly also defined conceptually and contextually as a result of a metadiscourse. Such a metadiscourse would be as a result of, but not limited to, a discussion on what it is to 'understand' within the discussion of what it is to 'communicate'.

> 'What a friend we have in Jesus':
> "What a Friend we have in Jesus,
> All our sins and griefs to bear!
> What a privilege to carry
> Everything to God in prayer!
> O what peace we often forfeit,
> O what needless pain we bear,
> All because we do not carry
> Everything to God in prayer!
> Have we trials and temptations?
> Is there trouble anywhere?
> We should never be discouraged,
> Take it to the Lord in prayer.
> Can we find a friend so faithful
> Who will all our sorrows share?
> Jesus knows our every weakness,
> Take it to the Lord in prayer.
> Are we weak and heavy-laden,
> Cumbered with a load of care?
> Precious Saviour, still our refuge—
> Take it to the Lord in prayer;
> Do thy friends despise, forsake thee?

Take it to the Lord in prayer;
In His arms He'll take and shield thee,
Thou wilt find a solace there."

This hymn, as an introduction to the theme, is an isolated example of the aphorism '*lex orandi, lex credendi,* and *lex (con)vivendi*'. Immediately there are multiple examples of the song writer, Joseph Scriven's, idea(s) of prayer (*lex orandi*), which both illustrates and is illustrated by his beliefs (*lex credendi*), while the plural 'we' suggests an idea of being church within and beyond the worship service (*lex (con)vivendi*). In a world where communication is abundant, especially with the ever expanding and thriving realm of social media which provides an opportunity for being church 'online', prayer is another form of communication.[6] It is a form of communication between believers in addition to being between believer (or believers) and God. Prayer undoubtedly forms an massive part of the liturgy in a worship service and the Church is known to be a hospital for sinners not a museum for saints. This hospital, so to speak, should be overflowing due to the nature of the world and all its problems. Continuing with this metaphor, hospitals are places of healing, and healing can be achieved through various forms and elements of therapy. Thus, to provide an example, therapy can come in the form of a ritual within the worship service—the efficacy of which could depend on the inclusivity, unity and 'being church' that a worshipper experiences in the worship service.

Included in the outcomes and the suggested theory for praxis is the therapeutic dimensions of prayer with the intent of creating a space for healing, which could also be seen as reconciliation, through inclusivity, unity or 'being church' together. There is a psychology behind prayer which will be described using empirical data and using theory from the fields of psychology and sociology. Whilst taking into consideration the perceptions, or beliefs, people have of God as observed by what they believe and how they pray.

Another of the outcomes is evident throughout this book, it proved advantageous to expand the field of study beyond Liturgical Studies to include a range of other disciplines. Thus, a strong case is made for interdisciplinary research. Investigations were not limited to the field of Liturgical Studies, the following fields were also included: Practical Theology—including its facets such as Pastoral Care and Homiletics, Cultural Anthropology—mainly including Ritual Studies, Systematic Theological

---

6. Barnard et al., *Worship in the network culture*.

Introduction

Ecclesiology, Psychology and Sociology. Although Liturgical Studies is the overarching field of study here, prayer is examined through the lenses of each of the abovementioned fields as well before a theory for praxis is suggested from a liturgical perspective in response to a calling from Pastoral Care and the notion of being church. This calling is made, in part, from Pastoral Care whilst likewise being illustrated in a statement made by Abigail Van Buren in 1964: "A church is not a museum for saints—it's a hospital for sinners." Typically, hospitals are spaces for healing, and the healing of a person not necessary physically but holistically is of great importance to Pastoral Care. A secondary reason for making use of this quotation is because, with inference, a hospital is a place of healing for all people therefore it is inherently inclusive. Thus a suggestion could be made that being church involves healing together, encompassed by the notion of *lex (con)vivendi*. Along with this suggestion is the notion that aspects of Pastoral Care involved in this ideal form part of being church.

Although prayer can be seen as a form of communication, it is not necessarily always a conversation. Prayer can also be a state of reverence, a time of meditation and contemplation. According to Barnard, Cilliers and Wepener, however, prayer does presume that someone—in this case God—is being addressed.[7][8] This is dependant on what is believed and how liturgy, prayer and worship are understood as well as how all of these function in different contexts. Prayer is not limited to Christians, or members of any faith in actuality. Non-Christians also have perceptions of the identity of God, there may not be a relationship, there may not even be a belief in God but some such people are capable of requesting people to pray. As an example, this illuminates that such people at least perceive God to be a last resort.

The beliefs of worshippers (*lex credendi*) and their interpretation of their beliefs is the subject, thus the act of prayer (*lex orandi*) is the object. By exploring the act of prayer in a pluralistic setting it was possible to develop a theory on a specific group's beliefs in today's society. This theory will be used for the *liturgia condenda* or 'liturgy in the making' and therefore also as a part of the liturgical praxis theory with regard to prayer.

---

7. Barnard et al., *Worship in the network culture*, 356–59.

8. Barnard et al., *Worship in the network culture*, 356–59. The authors explain a few different types of prayer (petitionary, penitence and thanksgiving and praise) and how there is a relationship involved in each of them. As well as how it affects both parties.

The Republic of South Africa is a country blessed with the richness and epitome of cultural diversity including vivid examples of cultural differences. These examples include but are most definitely limited to: apartheid, xenophobia, historical battles such as the Anglo-boer war(s) (also known as the South African war), the Anglo-Zulu war as well as the tyranny of King Shaka and the Zulu people. South Africa boasts a large number of official languages, typically each language comes with its own cultures and subcultures. The last census conducted in South Africa, in 2011, listed twelve languages and an 'Other' category. These languages are: Afrikaans (13,5percent), English (9,6percent), IsiNdebele (2,1 percent), IsiXhosa (16 percent), IsiZulu (22,7 percent), Sepedi (9,1 percent), Sesotho (7,6 percent), Setswana (8 percent), Sign Language, SiSwati (2,6 percent), Tshivenda (2,4 percent) and Xitsonga (4,5 percent).[9] With the effects of urbanisation the larger urban areas, and metropolitans, in South Africa are home to people of each of the abovementioned languages. With this in mind, the intention is to focus on one of the larger cities in South Africa where more popular liturgical cultures can be considered and then observe the cultures and the traditions, as well as the beliefs that come with these cultures and traditions. The back and forth conversations were examined between the traditions of the church and the cultures and traditions of people within those churches.

To date in a postapartheid era, since the birth of democracy in 1994, South Africans are still learning to live together (*lex (con)vivendi*), inclusively and in unity. The context of a new republic born out of the end of apartheid reveals concerns from South African people in general as well as from various fields of study. Considering reconciliation there are shared concerns over the restoration of broken relationships and inherited and inherent distain between race groups, cultures, economic statuses, education levels and those with various levels of privilege or previous disadvantage. All of which can be found in pluralistic urban areas, thus this urban area as one of the larger metropolitan areas was used as a microcosm of the South African context of diversity. This excluded some other forms of diversity for example the differences between urban and rural areas. These areas are diverse in the sense that some people in rural areas live without electricity while those in urban areas have seldom had the opportunity to go without it. This makes for extreme and incomparable observations which reaffirmed the choice of using an urban microcosm.

---

9. StatsSA, *Census 2011*, 23–27.

Introduction

Within this chosen urban area there is the context of diversity of languages, cultures and individuals that are in relation with one another. Within this city the majority of people are able to communicate in English without it being their first or even second language. There are also a variety of economic statuses, an environment of development in many sense of the word and a Christian context that shares similar theological points of departure in general. In and amongst the variety of differences are similarities shared between urbanites that are quite literally living together. Within an urban area there is a pluralistic, heterogenous population that is both learning and learnt to co-exist, there are spaces where cultures and languages are married and shared both within and outside of the church. This co-existence can, and has already been, referred to as living together, or *lex (con)vivendi*. The efficacy of living together has an effect of how people within this microcosm are 'being church'. The causal interrelationship made it possible to determine whether the liturgy was inculturated or not for those 'being church' (*lex (con)vivendi*) by examining both prayer (*lex orandi*) and, as a result, belief (*lex credendi*).

The basis of the approach for the research conducted throughout this project was Osmer's core tasks of practical theological interpretation. These four core tasks served as a guideline to follow throughout the project and provided some useful route markers for the core subjects in most of the chapters in this book. Osmer's four core tasks are: (1) the descriptive-empirical task, (2) the interpretive task, (3) the normative task, and (4) the pragmatic task. With each of these core tasks is an associated question that assists with each step of the research process. The reason behind using Osmer's core tasks of practical theological interpretation is due to the qualitative nature in which the research was conducted: "Qualitative research seeks to understand the actions and practices in which individuals and groups engage in everyday life and the meanings they ascribe to their experience."[10] Due to the nature of qualitative research being about the actions and practices of people, individually or in groups, the word 'describe' or 'description' appears regularly in academic literature.[11] The descriptive element of qualitative research aligns itself well with the first task mentioned above, namely the descriptive-empirical task. The same literature explains that with describing the actions, or what is going on, comes interpreting

---

10. Osmer, *Practical Theology*, 49.

11. Babbie and Mouton, *The Practice of Social Research*, 53–58; Miller-McLemore, *The Wiley-Blackwell Companion to Practical Theology*, 137–39.

or understanding these actions or practices. In this regard, the second and third tasks guide one on how to interpret and what interpretive tools to use. The final task, the pragmatic task, involves determining a response—in this case a new theory for praxis. Overall, Osmer's core tasks are an ideal guideline for the research approach of this project.

There were two initial, investigatory, questions that ought to be asked in order to be understand the main research problem. The first question was: what beliefs are exhibited by the worship manuals? And the second question was: what beliefs are exhibited by peoples' prayers? The first question considered fixed, rehearsed and/or prepared prayers, for example The Lord's Prayer or even The Benediction. The second question referred more to extemporaneous prayers, prayers that are more often said in one's private capacity for example; the type of prayer a mother and child would say while kneeling at the bed side. The ritual example of kneeling at the bed side is used as an example to show that prayer is not just an oral exercise but an overall bodily action; perhaps involving the simple bowing of heads or even the joining of hands in a congregation or around the family dinner table. Extemporaneous prayers, in the context of people's prayers, include spontaneous prayers such as in a charismatic church that does not follow as strict of a liturgical structure as the Anglican Church, for example. Both types of prayer, in- and outside of the church, are liturgical and of a ritual nature, they are diverse as they are performed by individuals—each and every one of them unique. Their uniqueness is a matrix of factors including, but not limited to, culture; language; race; city/province/country of origin, age, gender and perhaps even health to mention but a few factors.

The qualitative empirical components of the research project were done within Centurion, which forms part of the greater City of Tshwane municipality in the Gauteng Province of the Republic of South Africa. The ideal situation was to conduct said research at one higher liturgical congregation (for example a Roman Catholic or Anglican Church), one mainline congregation (for example a Methodist or Baptist Church) and then one charismatic church. The cultural contexts within the congregations should be South African, in the way that each congregation will have a variety of subcultures, revealing a community of diversity. If the context mentioned above is Western, Christian South Africans then the subcultures (mentioned in the previous sentence) could vary from black, isiZulu speaking South Africans—not only isiZulu speaking but being involved in Zulu culture—to white (Caucasian), Portuguese speaking South Africans. In both

Introduction

of these examples are South African people who are Christian, each has its own culture within the larger culture being examined—therefore a subculture. These subcultures influence a person's beliefs within the larger South African Christian cultural context. In other words, each subculture—in the diverse country of South Africa—has its own context. The main cultural context under the microscope will be the western church culture and not, for example—the African Independent Church context.

A short preview of the cultural and linguistic contexts has been given, both of these contexts have various methods of communication. The reason these contexts came to the fore was due to prayer being examined as a form of communication. Prayer, or praying, as a form of communication with people and/or with God is not the only topic going to be discussed, as a precursor the further validity of examining prayer, through qualitative empirical research will now be discussed in terms of the interrelationships of *lex orandi, lex credendi, lex (con)vivendi* in order to better understand how prayer, its form and content, impacts the ways in which people connect with God and other people. Below is a table of how many times the word 'pray' appears in different translations of the Bible:

Table 1: Use of the word 'pray' in different translations of the Bible		
Translation	Old Testament	New Testament
King James Version	245	68
New American Standard Version 1995 ed.	57	52
New International Version	48	73
New Revised Standard Version	61	61

'Pray' is one of 28 words on a list of frequently used words in the Bible. It is clearly not mentioned the most, however the fact that this word made it onto the list shows two things: (1) It is a word that is clearly mentioned many times in the Bible(s); and (2) that it is something of concern to many people who asked the question "how many times does the word 'pray' appear in the Bible?", thus explaining why it was of enough relevance to place on this list as a frequently asked question (or FAQ). It is relevant to mention, without delving into the field of Biblical Studies, that there is a causal relationship between prayer (*lex orandi*) and belief (*lex credendi*) illustrated in the Bible as noted by Smit who describes that the disciples learnt to pray through Jesus' example and these prayers were of the utmost importance to the early church as a guideline, model, norm of how to truly pray—but also how to truly believe and therefore live. From a different viewpoint, one from outside of the church, the above explains how important and/or relevant prayer and praying is to the Christian faith. It is mentioned, suggested and instructed a varying numbers of times in different translations of the Bible and also that it is a popular question to ask, not only answering the direct question but also the indirect question of how important prayer or praying is to Christianity in terms of belief and living—the answer given by the direct question answers or alludes to the indirect question.

As mentioned previously, prayer is a form of communication. Communication gives an indication of how one person feels about another—if one person is fond of another, one will speak to them with respect and fondness. That is just one of many examples that can be given. How one 'speaks' to God in and through prayer will give an indication of how a person or people perceive God. God takes many different forms for different people, example of this include Jesus as: Shepherd, Teacher, Witness, Redeemer, Counsellor and Deliverer. All of the above labels or similes exist because of different perceptions people have of God. The perceptions that they have are a sign of their needs from the liturgy and God. These needs clearly differ and may be from a group of people (a culture) or simply from individual to individual.

To summarise this introductory chapter, revision of the critical aspects of the research will be provided in retrospect of the contexts that have been described and discussed above. The main question of this research project is: how does the form and content of prayer impact the ways in which people connect with God and other people? This alludes to additional questions that aid in answering the original, main research question which are:

- How do people communicate with God? Prayer is one important answer, which is why the manner in which people pray was investigated through semi-structured interviews and observations of Sunday worship services.

- Why do people pray, both as a congregation in the worship service and in one's private capacity? Prayer, similarly to the point above, is the object of this question therefore the reasons behind why people pray was investigated by means of semi-structured interviews.

- What do people pray about and what are the reasons behind their prayers? This was investigated through the semi-structured

INTRODUCTION

interviewing of worshippers as well as through participatory observations.

The research questions that are listed above, are purely as a result of the research aims. These questions are not new, they are however being asked from a new context—an interdisciplinary one. The questions above are not being asked to prove anything from a psychological perspective, nor a sociological one. Prayer is a religious and ritual phenomenon, it is enjoyable to some; a calling card in times of crises to others. In this sense, an investigation is being made from a liturgical, ritual and Pastoral Care perspective, leaning heavily on the theory and praxis of liturgical inculturation in order to develop a theory that satisfies the main research question below. The research gap and question left by it is as a result of asking the above questions from the perspective described above. In similar fashion to the questions above, which were formulated as a result of the main research question, the aims of this research project are listed below. The research aims are:

- To determine if people perceive they can connect with God and fellow worshippers through prayer, within their diverse, cultural context(s) and if so how they connect.
- To develop a new theory for praxis that allows the congregation to connect with God in prayer through their cultural-liturgical and cultural-ritual contexts—where diversity meets familiarity.

At this point it should be mentioned that similar studies have been conducted, albeit from different perspectives and/or methods. This includes as examples: Smit conducted literary research and not empirical, Wepener, who considered reconciliation rituals and on eating but not specifically prayer, Van Wyk approached the challenge of 'being church' in the twenty-first century from a Trinitarian-ecclesiological perspective with systematic theology, Pieterse focussed on homiletics, van Ommen considered Pastoral Care and liturgical formation, Rossouw focussed on racial inclusivity in the Dutch Reformed Church, Van Deusen Hunsinger wrote on practicing *koinonia*, Ackermann wrote existentially on a relationship ethic of difference and otherness, de Klerk and Kruger wrote on the influence social cognition has on liturgical formation, Fuist conducted empirical research on 'collective' prayer, Crawford and Best considered koinonia and worship from an ecumenical perspective, Baker investigated the sociological patterns of prayer frequency and content, Tarascar focussed on the churches' search for koinonia from an ecumenical perspective, James Baesler and Chen researched the domain of digital petitionary prayer, Krause examined the relationship between prayer expectancies, race and self-esteem in the elderly and Van der Borght conducted a literary analysis of three documents that discussed reconciliation and healing and focussed on the past link between church and ethnicity.

The reason for this research project was due to a recognised gap in the research field. Prayer as a phenomenon has been studied and discussed by the fields of psychology and philosophy. Prayer as an element of Christianity has been examined, hermeneutically, from a New Testament Studies perspective; revealing why prayers such as The Lord's Prayer are prayed and what specific prayers mean. It has also been examined from a liturgical, practical theological, perspective as an example: within the context of appropriation and appreciation for both worshippers and worship leaders. The gap, when researching prayer, is primarily from a liturgical perspective, especially when considering the wide variety of cultural contexts (especially the cultural diversity in pluralistic cities) that are worshipping at a single worship service. This gap leaves a question: does the tradition of the church allow its entire congregation to pray in a manner that their cultures can understand and relate to completely? As an example: does the tradition of the Anglican Church allow its entire congregation, among them being speakers of all the official languages of South Africa, to pray (both prayers out of the Anglican prayer book and extemporaneous prayers) in a manner that their cultures (influenced by their mother tongue) can understand and relate to completely (connect with)?

This connection, understanding and/or relationship was explained by Chupungco, who uses a metaphor to explain the relationship: if one were to burn a candle from both ends, one end being the wants (culturally or otherwise) of the congregation and the other being the liturgical tradition of the church, the two ends would eventually meet.[12] The word 'meet' can be manipulated or understood as 'connect'. In the city of Centurion, at the participating Methodist church for example, there is an exquisite array of cultures sitting in a single worship service. All of these 'cultures' (as people) arrive at the church expecting to communicate with God, to connect with their fellow worshippers. So, on the one end of the candle are the wants not only of one culture, as the case would be in more rural areas of the country,

---

12. Chupungco, *Liturgical Inculturation*.

Introduction

but of many cultures under one roof. Each culture, in its own right longing for a place of worship where it can connect with God and worship fully.

In conclusion, the research project served to develop a theory based on the main question asked above. The concluding chapter is not only a conclusion but also a pragmatically developed response that suggests a new theory for praxis that serves as *liturgia condenda*, or liturgy in the making, through liturgical inculturation. In terms of liturgical inculturation this should be done by ensuring that the two ends of the candle meet in the, proverbial, middle and not more towards the one end nor the other. In other words there should be equal input and consideration from both the 'wants' of the congregation, culturally speaking , and the liturgical tradition of the church. Culture being that which forms part of one'w heritage and not popular culture (or pop culture). Therefore the churches' prayer traditions should meet the worshippers beliefs, consisting of both church tradition and cultural elements, in the middle so that all in the worship service are being church—or are worshipping (living) together. This would, thereby, unite and aid those in feeling inclusively part of the worship service in terms of *lex orandi, lex credendi, lex (con)vivendi*.

Chapter 1

KEY CONCEPTS

THERE ARE FOUR KEY concepts that will be explored throughout, namely liturgy which includes prayer; ritual which includes ritualization; church, including the marks of the church; and unity, as well as inclusivity. However, due to the interdisciplinary approach taken there are a handful of concepts that relate to the key concepts. For instance the field of Liturgical Studies is a subdiscipline within the broader field of Practical Theology. Nevertheless it is important to delve into the epistemology that led to this research being conducted. As a precursor it is necessary to begin with an understanding of Practical Theology.

1.1. PRACTICAL THEOLOGY AS A FIELD OF STUDY

Schleiermacher was of the understanding that all studies of Theology are defined by their relationships to the life of the church, therefore Theology lives from its subject matter.[1] According to Miller-McLemore Practical Theology has four distinctive meanings: (1) Way of life: Shaping faith among believers in home and society, (2) Method: Studying theology in practice in library and field, (3) Curriculum: Educating for ministry and faith in classroom, congregation and community, and (4) Discipline: Defining history and context in guild and global setting.[2]

---

1. Gräb, *Practical Theology as theology of religion*, 181–96.
2. Miller-McLemore, *The Wiley-Blackwell Companion to Practical Theology*, 6–13.

Key Concepts

Therefore, according to Miller-Mclemore, Practical Theology can be defined as "shaping faith among believers, studying theology in practice, educating for ministry and defining content and method."[3] Similarly Heitink defines, as a theory of action, Practical Theology as: "the empirically orientated theological theory of mediation of the Christian faith in the praxis of modern society."[4] This definition can be understood by distinguishing between two different concepts: "the mediation of Christian faith (praxis 1)" and "the praxis of modern society (praxis 2)." The first concept of praxis "indicates that the unique concept of Practical Theology is related to intentional, more intermediary or mediative, actions, with a view to changing a given situation through agogics." While the second concept of this praxis "emphasises the context, where these actions take place, as a dynamic context in which men and women in society interact."

A working definition of Practical Theology as study field can be suggested: Practical Theology aims to shape the Christian faith in its modern, albeit it dynamic, context through mediation by studying theology and religious practice—literary and empirically, thereby educating the ministry, congregation and community through the development of praxis. This working definition can be given, based on the above definitions of Practical Theology. Osmer claims no originality in the terms of describing the tasks of practical theological interpretation. He also admits that similar concepts are taught in the academy and ministry. Osmer's approach to practical theological interpretation was found most appropriate for this research, which is described here and is congruent with the working definition provided above. Osmer uses the term practical theological interpretation to indicate corollaries of his central argument regarding the fourfold nature of Practical Theology: "(1) practical theological interpretation takes place in all specialised subdisciplines of Practical Theology; (2) the same structure of practical theological interpretation in academic Practical Theology characterises the interpretive tasks of congregational leaders as well; (3) acknowledging the common structure of practical theological interpretation in both the academy and ministry can help congregational leaders recognise the interconnectedness of ministry."[5]

Heitink notes that the "practical" can be seen as the opposite of the "theoretical", however the object (of inquiry) of Practical Theology is the

---

3. Miller-McLemore, *The Wiley-Blackwell Companion to Practical Theology*, 6.

4. Heitink, *Practical Theology*, 6.

5. Osmer, *Practical Theology*, 12.

theory of praxis.⁶ Therefore the object of Practical Theology, and its subdisciplines, is action or activity. This study's objects of inquiry were the actions and activities of prayer and belief. In terms of interpreting these actions and activities, Osmer's four task structure was deemed appropriate in this case. In his structure of practical theological interpretation, Osmer refers to the terms 'episodes', 'situations' and 'contexts' rather than Heitink's 'action' and 'activity'.⁷ The structure of practical theological interpretation, provided by Osmer, begins by (1) describing the scene—what is going on; then (2) interpreting the revealed episodes, situations and contexts (including actions and activities) through various arts and sciences; followed by (3) interpreting episodes, situations and contexts by using theological concepts; finally (4) responding by determining theories for praxis. This structure is appropriate because of its precise, step-by-step approach to practical theological interpretation.

1.1.1. The Field of Liturgical Studies

Further justification for the use of Osmer's model of practical theological interpretation is that it is applicable to the specialised subdisciplines of Practical Theology. Liturgical Studies is a subdiscipline of Practical Theology. Liturgical Studies, or liturgical theology, is a subdiscipline of Practical Theology that studies "the particular ways in Christian worship is formative and expressive of a Christian way of life."⁸

An explanation was provided above which understands that the object of Practical Theology is the theory of praxis. As a subdiscipline of Practical Theology, Liturgical Studies is likewise concerned with the ways in which theory and praxis are integrated into the research design. This further serves as motivation for the appropriate use of Osmer's model of practical theological interpretation, which considers the interpretation of various theories in tasks two and three so that a pragmatic response can be formed. Before proceeding, it is important to provide a working definition of liturgy as it is understood in this book:

> Liturgy is the encounter between God and man in which God and man move out towards one another, a movement in which

---

6. Heitink, *Practical Theology*, 7.
7. Osmer, *Practical Theology*, 12.
8. Miller-McLemore, *The Wiley-Blackwell Companion to Practical Theology*, 290.

Key Concepts

> God's action is primacy, so that in a theonomic reciprocal fashion a dialogical communication in and through rituals and symbols is established in which man participates in a bodily way and can in this reach his [or her] highest goal in life, namely to praise God and enjoy Him forever.[9]

There are various approaches to Liturgical Studies, all of which can be divided into three broad areas: "liturgical history, liturgical theology and liturgy as ritual/symbolic event."[10] It was noted previously that prayer is a religious and ritual phenomenon, therefore this study approaches the field from the perspective of "liturgy as ritual/symbolic event." In terms of understanding liturgy as ritual and symbolic events, Wepener provides an example for approaching Liturgical Studies from the understanding that liturgy involves ritual by proposing the following: "If the liturgy is understood as a complex web of Christian rituals and symbols, and rituals and symbols are seen as the building blocks of the liturgy, then approaches from disciplines with similar interests (also taking symbols and rituals as objects of research) might be of value."[11]

Approaching this liturgical study from a historical point of departure would be to develop a historical understanding of the liturgy, which would be an erroneous approach to gaining insight into the research question. The aims of the historical investigation of liturgy, as illustrated by Schattauer, are an indication as to why such an approach would be in vain:

> The principal aims of the historical investigation of liturgy have been (1) to uncover the origins of the principal rites (e.g., Eucharist, baptism, daily prayer, Easter vigil) and usages (e.g., calendar and lectionary) and to trace their development through time; (2) to distinguish the classical liturgical families of Eastern and Western Christianity and the various Protestant traditions of worship; and (3) to a lesser extent, to reconstruct the worship of particular communities at a given time and place.[12]

The research problem, and question, is concerned with the present by asking: how does the form and content of prayer impact the ways in which people connect with God and other people? Hence, this study could not assume a liturgical history approach to the object of inquiry. Perhaps

---

9. Wepener, *From Fast to Feast*, 21.
10. Schattauer, *Liturgical Studies*, 106.
11. Wepener, *Researching Rituals*, 110.
12. Schattauer, *Liturgical Studies*, 108.

more, albeit not completely, appropriate than a liturgical history approach is a liturgically theological approach as it involves theological reflection in relation to liturgical practice, past and present. A liturgical theology approach involves theological fields such as eschatology and systematics, and presupposed liturgy as theology. Although liturgical theology is concerned with the reflection of present and past liturgical practice which is a concern of this study, it is not the point of departure of this study. The reason for this is that this study is concerned with the actions and activities, in other words the rituals and symbolic events of worshipping and praying.

This study took a liturgical-ritual approach as it considers the liturgy as a complex web of Christian rituals and symbols. These rituals and symbols are seen as the building blocks of the liturgy. Liturgy, or worship and prayer, is dialogical communication in and through these building blocks. Worship and prayer are activities, which are "a set of practices, experiences and fundamental dispositions towards what is deemed most sacred."[13] As such worship is practical, liturgy is a complex web of ritual actions and symbolic activities that can be categorised into episodes, situations and contexts. These ritual and symbolic episodes, situations, contexts and their protagonists—the worshippers—both form and are formed by the liturgy.

By taking a liturgical-ritual approach the object(s) of inquiry becomes the ritual actions and symbolic activities, therefore when researching rituals it is important to document the enactment of rituals as well as the appropriation of rituals by participants. This, once more, substantiates the choice for using Osmer's model and structure of practical theological interpretation as most appropriate, from a liturgical-ritual point of departure. To examine ritual actions and symbolic activities is to sub-textually ask, 'what is going on?', which is the question associated with the first task of practical theological interpretation. Furthermore, the validity of using Osmer's four task structure lies in the process of the second and third tasks of practical theological interpretation. These tasks implicitly approach the aforementioned episodes, situations and contexts from liturgical theology and, to a lesser extent, liturgical history.

Osmer's model, or structure, is a dynamic hermeneutical circle or spiral which means that the four tasks are distinct, however they are also connected.[14] This allows for appropriate inclusions of liturgical history and

---

13. Miller-McLemore, *The Wiley-Blackwell Companion to Practical Theology*, 290.

14. Osmer, *Practical Theology*, 23; Smith, *Review of Richard Osmer, Practical Theology*, 101.

liturgical theology approaches, within a liturgical-ritual approach. Due to prayer being the determined object of inquiry, this study took a predominantly liturgical-ritual approach as it examined prayer actions and activities as rituals and symbols. However, by conducting the study in terms of Osmer's four task structure, it allowed for the approach to dynamically shift, if and when necessary to a liturgical history and/or liturgical theology approach. Examining and interpreting liturgical rituals, from a liturgical-ritual approach, should entail considering theories from the field of Ritual Studies in addition to liturgical sources of theory. An alliance between the fields of Liturgical Studies and rituals studies has been formed, such an alliance is an example of interdisciplinarity. Therefore it is important to discuss the concept of interdisciplinary studies.

1.2. INTERDISCIPLINARITY

An alliance, for example, between Liturgical Studies and Ritual Studies illustrates an approach from interdisciplinary studies. What makes interdisciplinary studies unique is the approach to integrate separate theories from different disciplines, arts and/or sciences. By integrating theories from Liturgical Studies and Ritual Studies, as suggested by the aforementioned alliance between the two, new knowledge can emerge by means of (re)defining the relationship of the disciplines, developing integrative concepts and generating unconventional insights. However there are other processes of inquiry that involve multiple disciplinary study. One such approach is multidisciplinary studies, which juxtaposes disciplinary and professional perspectives, adding breadth and available knowledge, information and methods. These additions speak as separate voices in encyclopaedic alignment. In other words, wider knowledge of a subject is developed through a greater number of inputs. Immediately, the difference between interdisciplinary and multidisciplinary studies is the relationship between disciplines. Interdisciplinary approaches integrate, or marry, disciplinary theories, data, concepts and methods to create a more holistic views. Whereas multidisciplinary approaches use disciplinary theories, et cetera, to add to the knowledge pool, however these disciplines maintain their separate identities.

Another approach is that of transdisciplinary studies, explanations of which vary from a set of common postulations that transcend the narrow scope of disciplinary worldviews through an overarching merge to the critical evaluation of terms, concepts and methods that transgress disciplinary boundaries.[15] The core trend of transdisciplinarity, which is prominent in Europe, is that problems in the world of lived experience are needed to frame research questions and practices and not problems in the disciplines. Therefore, it can be explained that transdisciplinarity overlooks the borders of disciplines and focusses on an individual discipline—the *Lebenswelt* (or "lifeworld").[16]

A definition of interdisciplinarity, illustrated by its key concepts, is helpful in understanding an alliance between different disciplines. The integrated definition of interdisciplinarity, which illustrates its key concepts, below should aid in motivating the use of such an approach:

- Interdisciplinary research has a particular substantive focus.
- The focus of interdisciplinary research extends beyond a single disciplinary perspective.
- A distinctive characteristics of interdisciplinary research is that it focusses on a problem that is complex.
- Interdisciplinary research is characterised by an identifiable process or mode of inquiry.
- Interdisciplinary research draws explicitly on the disciplines.
- The disciplines provide insight about the specific substantive focus of interdisciplinary research.
- Interdisciplinary research has integration as its goal.
- The objective of interdisciplinary research process is pragmatic: to produce a cognitive advancement in the form of a new understanding, a new product or a new meaning.[17]

The points illustrated above add further motivations not only for using the structure but also the concept(s) of interdisciplinary studies. There is an alliance between Liturgical Studies and Ritual Studies which, as explained above, presupposes interdisciplinary studies due to the relationship between theories of the two disciplines being integrated to form new knowledge and insights. Therefore, when considering liturgical rituals there is a cause to take an interdisciplinary approach. An interdisciplinary

---

15. Lunsford et al., *The rhetoric of interdisciplinarity*, 280–81.
16. Lunsford et al., *The rhetoric of interdisciplinarity*, 281.
17. see Repko and Szostak, *The interdisciplinary research process*, 10.

approach was taken because of the intention to integrate theories from various arts and science as well as different theological disciplines to develop new understandings of the form and content of prayer. In reference to the key concepts of interdisciplinarity above, the following concepts aid in motivating the use of interdisciplinarity: "The focus of interdisciplinary research extends beyond a single disciplinary perspective" and "A distinctive characteristics of interdisciplinary research is that it focusses on a problem that is complex."[18] As an example, later in the book there are liturgical-ritual interpretations. This involved integrated ritual theories into perspectives from Liturgical Studies. There are also ritual-liturgical interpretations which, similarly, interpreted from the perspective of Ritual Studies whilst integrating theories from the field of Liturgical Studies.

1.3. THE KEY CONCEPTS

This research project began with empirical data collection by means of qualitative research methods. In order to analyze and interpret the collected data, there needed to be clarity on the key concepts employed throughout the research project. As there are always certain conscious and/or unconscious assumptions behind every choice, meaning that specific questions and methodology used to collect empirical data represent the first steps toward interpretation. Therefore the use of some of the key concepts below began in the formative stages of the research project, this includes the research design. Below are descriptions of the key concepts used throughout the research process.

1.3.1. Liturgy

As explained in the earlier section which discussed Liturgical Studies as a field, the term 'liturgy' is understood by Wepener's working definition: "Liturgy is the encounter between God and man in which God and man move out towards one another, a movement in which God's action is primacy, so that in a theonomic reciprocal fashion a dialogical communication in and through rituals and symbols is established in which man participates in a bodily way and can in this reach his [or her] highest goal in life, namely to

---

18. Repko and Szostak, *The interdisciplinary research process*, 10.

praise God and enjoy Him forever."[19] Concerned with how the form and content of prayer impact the ways in which people connect with God and other people it is imperative to describe the phenomenon of prayer and how it is understood here.

Prayer differs from worship in the sense that Christian worship includes prayer as liturgical-ritual, however it does not necessarily involve praying. As a result of this, prayer is approached from two different interdisciplinary perspectives: firstly from a ritual-liturgical perspective which approaches prayer from a Ritual Studies perspective and integrates theory from Liturgical Studies and secondly from a Liturgical Studies perspective which approaches prayer as a liturgical construct and integrates theory from Ritual Studies. Therefore prayer is seen both as a ritual act and as an act included by liturgy.

1.3.1.1. Prayer

It was explained, using the aphorism *lex orandi, lex credendi, lex (con)vivendi*, that there is an interrelationship between prayer, belief and living together. Prayer can be seen as a liturgical-ritual act, performed within and outside of the worship service. From a liturgical perspective prayer, as a ritual, often involves worship but worship does not necessarily include prayer. Brümmer distinguished three different types of ritual prayer: petitionary prayers, penitential prayers and thanksgiving prayers.[20] As a liturgical ritual, in the worship service prayer can be explained as petitioning God to come down in our acts of worship. However, below is a working definition of prayer:

As a phenomenon, prayer is a communicative ritual. Prayer communicates expressions of need and affirmations of faith. Expressions of need can be communicated through prayer in expectation of improving one's wellbeing—or self. In such cases prayer is as a response to a need. The motivation for, or purpose of praying, is that it has an impact on the one praying and/or being prayed for. Christian prayer is an intimate form of communication, whether verbal or contemplative, with a benevolent and loving God.

Again, there was and still is a concern over how the form and content of prayer impact the ways in which people connect with God and other people. The key concept of liturgical inculturation plays an important role

---

19. Wepener, *From Fast to Feast*, 21.
20. Brümmer, *What are we doing when we pray*, 74.

Key Concepts

in not only understanding the research problem but also in the development of a theory for praxis.

1.3.1.2. Liturgical Inculturation

Simply defined liturgical inculturation is "a continuous process of critical-reciprocal interaction between cult (liturgy) and culture so that a totally new entity comes into being, namely an inculturated liturgy."[21] This definition is similar to the analogy created by Chupungco. Both look at either ends of the stick, or candle, and create ways for them to meet. Culture has to meet with cult in order for believers to connect fully to what is going on. However, in any of the three churches mentioned above there is not just one culture, there are many. From attending the services and obtaining what statistics were available, it is difficult to state if there is a single culture that has majority in any of the churches. Chupungco refers to 'wants' whereas Wepener refers to 'culture' in the same context.

There are layered contexts to the ritual data as well as the ritual-liturgical relationship(s) between the tradition(s) of the church(es) and the culture(s) of worshippers, all of which influence the concept of being church. As explained there are a multiplicity of cultures in each of these churches, one main contributing factor being urbanisation. There is a 'layer' of overall culture, below that layer is a matrix of cultures, not merely a single culture. Thus liturgical interculturation , as a facet of liturgical inculturation, should be explored and remain in consideration throughout the process of this project and liturgical inculturation. The process of interculturation, within liturgical inculturation, can be described as multilateral traffic between theologies from across the world, but in a manner that the Global North does not remain the charitable nor the Global South a needy recipient, rather that all involved give and receive in order for all involved to be equally enriched through the process.

Like many other colonised countries, South Africa has a history of exclusion especially in light of the apartheid regime (pre-1994). It should be the role of the church, in present day South Africa, to ensure that all worshippers, whether they are members or guests feel included in the worship service. Liturgical interculturation is not a static process and neither should liturgical inculturation be. For the purpose of this project there was no immediate need to look all over the world but rather look at other

---

21. Wepener, *From Fast to Feast*, 42.

churches in the same context. Therefore the process described above has been adapted in the sense that the 'giving and receiving' is between the three churches; their traditions and the traditions of the people who attend the various services, all within the context of the City of Centurion, a city in the Republic of South Africa. The Nairobi Statement on Worship and Culture's introduction highlights the importance of liturgical inculturation and with it, liturgical interculturation by stating, among other important points, that worship is the heart and pulse of the Christian Church. If worship is the heart and pulse of the Christian Church, then surely total inclusion is of somewhat paramount importance—if a worshipper or group thereof is not connected to the worship service as there is no 'traffic' between their culture and the tradition of the church, then surely the church has no 'heart beat' for said worshipper(s).[22] The Nairobi Statement of course explains, importantly, that worship should relate counter-culturally to culture—not only in a consumeristic fashion. In this case liturgical interculturation can be done in a manner that authority is not shared between culture and liturgical tradition, in such a way that the liturgy still preserves some sense of exclusivity.

The influences of urbanisation suggest, and the retained presupposition, is that in any urban South African church there is no isolated culture, especially in the three churches where the research was conducted. All the believers can communicate in English, there they find a common ground. Each believer chose the specific church tradition of the church they attend, simply by attending it therein they find another common ground. Beyond either of these things is a complex matrix of differences, making each believer unique. The term, at least in its singular version, 'culture' is not one that which can be used to best describe the one end of the candle that needs to meet the other, being cult or liturgy. The term 'wants' is not preferable due to the fact that the connection that believers seek when attending a worship service is more vital. However, 'culture' or 'cultures' will be implemented as a blanket term as it best describes the complex aspects that culminate to determine someone's context, one's identity and the way in which one experiences the worship service. The reason for this being that each element, comprised of which is an individual, has its own culture or subculture, or better still societal dictations and trends. This is amplified by the concept of a network society, the world becoming a global village where immediate social action has taken the proverbial backseat to social

---

22. Lutheran World Federation, *Nairobi Statement*, 1.

forms and the power of flows or trends. As for culture (and Christianity), it means that "values and ideas are being circulated through world wide networks in which people participate interactively."[23] This in turn means that believers are not only connected to their immediate society, geographically speaking, but also to the network society that operates, in its many forms including social media and pop-culture, in a way that influences a believer beyond their immediate surroundings and culture.

For example, society (both immediate and network) suggests that a man (or gentleman) should behave a certain way; that a fully matured adult should behave a certain way. In the case of the network society, this could change depending on current trends and developments. A person's race, language and cultural background also make suggestions of how they should present themselves; understand certain things and behave in certain situations. Popular phrases such as 'real men don't cry', 'I'm not a child anymore' and 'that's not how you treat a lady' are all examples of how factors such as gender, age and culture dictate a person's understanding or context: how they see the world, how they want the world to see them and how they participate inclusively and exclusively in being church. The same could be said for the worship service and its facilitators, everyone wants to hear their favourite hymn and feel like the pastor, minister, reverend or priest is addressing them personally. Here lies the critical-reciprocal interaction in these multi-cultural churches and why the term 'culture' is somewhat misleading in terms of what is being examined throughout this project, albeit the best possible term that can be used.

The following understanding highlights three critical aspects of prayer in the worship service. Firstly, the connection between the individual and God; secondly, the relationships between individuals in the worship service being one congregation; and lastly, the relations between the congregation as a single entity and God. Although the three aspects are separated, there is also a fluidity between all three as a single concept that is more complex than the understanding of prayer as part of the worship service. To pray is to accept that you can comprehend your life only as an existence in relation with others and with God. Thus, to pray is a extremely cultural-critical act. Worshippers act through worship, prayer and song in expectation of God; who promised to come but who also tears down their autonomy and assembles them into a heteronomous relation with Him and each other.

---

23. Barnard, *Flows of worship in the network society*, 73.

This understanding of what it is to pray as well as the critical aspects mentioned, that allude to the aphorism 'as we pray, so we believe, so we live (together)', were kept in mind throughout the process of developing a new theory for praxis. However, the aim was not to develop a theory for praxis only for the relationship between the individual worshipper and God. Instead, the aim was to develop a theory for praxis that is inclusive of all three of the connections and/or relations referred to as critical aspects of prayer.

1.3.2. Ritual

The term 'ritual' can be defined, explained and understood in a number of ways. Due to there being no single origin of ritual there is no single explanation. Likewise, the study of ritual, in an ideal sense, starts with informed participation in—and observation of—ritual activity. Therefore, understandings, explanations and/or definitions of 'ritual' are not limited as a result of hermeneutics influenced by (informed) participation and observations of rituals. It is, however, necessary to provide an explanation or understanding of what ritual is in this context. As a result of the interdisciplinary nature of this exploration it was necessary to draw on theories from Ritual Studies experts, such as Ronald Grimes and Catherine Bell, as well as scholars from Liturgical Studies, such as Cas Wepener, Johan Cilliers and Marcel Barnard.

1.3.2.1. Defining Ritual

While scholars from the field of Ritual Studies discuss the variety of explanations of ritual, their definitions more often than not focus on explaining the functions and/or structures of ritual. From the field of Liturgical Studies, Wepener provided a more outright, albeit working definition of ritual(s):

> Rituals are often repeated, self-evident, symbolic actions, that are always interactive and corporeal, sometimes accompanied by texts and formulas, aimed at the transfer of values in the individual or the group, and of which the form and content are always culture, context and time bound, so that the involvement in the reality which is presented in the rituals remains dynamic.[24]

---

24. Wepener, *From Fast to Feast*, 36.

Typically the term ritual denotes a generalised scientific idea of what becomes reality in performing rites. There are then dimensions to ritual, each with certain qualities; bearing certain similarities however fundamentally different. Ritual then, as defined in above, includes rites, rites of passage and ritualization. A rite can be explained as a concrete, fixed pattern of activity at specific times in specific places, or choreographed actions that exist for the duration of their enactment after which they vanish. Rites of passage differ from rites or ritual practices. Rites of passage have the ability to transform the when enacted effectively, by carrying the participant(s) from one state to another in a way that they are unable to return to what was the status quo. The fundamental difference between rites and rites of passage is that the former is only performed while the later transforms. The momentous metamorphosis of a caterpillar in becoming a butterfly illustrates the intended transformation involved in a rite of passage, this transformation is only appropriated through effective rites of passage.

Briefly explained, ritualization can be understood as daily ritual behaviour as well as creating rituals in experimental and/or conscious ways. Also referred to as ritualising, ritualization can also be described as the act of intentionally cultivating or creating rites. Ritualization leads to the formation of rituals and therefore is presupposed in all other ritual modes such as liturgy.

With the understanding that this is no single explanation of ritual and given that explanations tend to focus on the functions and/or structure of ritual, Ronald Grimes provided a list of six modes of ritual that aid in both understanding and identifying ritual. This list includes: ritualization, decorum, ceremony, magic, liturgy and celebration.[25] This list was provided with the understanding that these categories flow into one another; they are interpenetrative and demand one another. As an example, there are celebration liturgies, ceremonial liturgies and decorous liturgies.

1.3.3. Ecclesiology

Expanding on the interdisciplinary approach, theory from the field of Ecclesiology was integrated to further develop new understandings. Therefore Ecclesiology, from Systematic Theological standpoint, is a key concept. Briefly explained, ecclesiology is the systematic study of the church.

---

25. Grimes, *Beginnings in Ritual Studies*, 47.

1.3.3.1. Ecclesiology in Systematic Theology

Ecclesiology initially gained an established standing in systematic theology during the Reformation, albeit a limited standing as many vital topics received little attention. As a separate locus, or field of study, ecclesiology gained prominence during the Middle Ages. Ecclesiology, as explained above, is the systematic study of the church. Therefore 'church' is understood as the tangible community where Christians congregate for worship, prayer, sharing, instruction, contemplation and mission; as one social organisation among many whilst also being viewed as a shared form of life moulded by earnest theological self-understandings. Therefore as a systematic study, the field of ecclesiology constitutes all of the interacting dimensions above. Ecclesiology, as a normative study of communities, examines the churches' forms of: "governance, liturgical life and corporate witness as primary instruments by which the Gospel is lived and communicated."[26] As a field of study, ecclesiology explores the concept and reality of 'church' by broadly formulating the social conditions of assertions of faith and then, explores the character of the self-understanding presented within these communal, organisational gatherings.

Mannion and Mudge explain that ecclesiology today asks "what sort of articulate communal expressions of faith will play the most significant roles in the complex human commonwealth now emerging on this planet."[27] According to Moltmann the church "stands for God to the world, and it stands for the world before God", therefore the church "will always have to present itself" in the forums of both God and the world.[28] The church, through Ecclesiological Studies, supplies an account to the world (humankind) of its "commission implicit in its faith" and the way in which it fulfils its duty. Therefore ecclesiology, as the systematic study of the church, involves the study of church doctrine. Moltmann describes four dimensions of doctrine of the church: (1) "The Church of Jesus Christ", (2) "The Missionary Church", (3) "The ecumenical church", and (4) "The Political Church."[29]

Similarly to Liturgical Studies there are various approaches to Ecclesiological Studies. Kärkkäinen describes four approaches: traditional

---

26. Mannion and Mudge, *The Routledge companion to the christian church*, 3
27. Mannion and Mudge, *The Routledge companion to the christian church*, 4.
28. Moltmann, *The church in the power of the spirit*, 1.
29. Moltmann, *The church in the power of the spirit*, 4–18.

ecclesiology, doctrinal ecclesiology and contextual ecclesiology.[30] Traditional ecclesiology approaches the church from a specific ecumenical perspective, usually related to specific denominations. A doctrinal approach is one that involves the understandings of specific doctrines voiced, in ecumenically sensitive manners, in contemporary theologians such as Zizioulas, Moltmann and Küng. Contextual ecclesiology concerns itself with the conditions of being church; whilst also examining, among others, feminist ecclesiologies; liberationist ecclesiology and the ecclesiologies of the African Independent Churches (AIC). Lastly, comparative ecclesiology draws from two kinds of sources: more or less official denominational confessional writings, and the texts of representative theologians.

The introductory chapter noted that consumerism played a potentially influential role in this research project as people have become more consumerised in the postmodern era. To better understand the postmodern challenges of ecclesiology, Mannion explains that human being and the main elements of being human have become commodities that can be picked, mixed, chosen and "bought", such as: sexuality, gender, religious and political affiliations.[31] This consumeristic era has enabled people to pick and mix from Christianity's doctrinal belief systems, pedagogy, liturgy, ways of living and ecclesial practices which means that Christianity and the church face a major challenge in protecting and promoting the place and mission of the faith community in the world. This challenge poses a fitting object of inquiry for postmodern ecclesiology, namely the relationship between the church and the world, which is not new to either the church or Christianity. Such an inquiry can be approached from opposing perspectives: world-affirming and world-renouncing, the former suggests openness and engagement with the world while the latter suggests inward ecclesial thinking, perceiving the church community's abdication of the world. These opposing perspectives are mentioned for the purposes of describing the postmodern challenges of ecclesiology, a debate of which will not be entered into. Instead, while on the subject of ecclesiology, discussions on the theory of 'church' are described.

---

30. Kärkkäinen, *An introduction to ecclesiology*, 12–14.
31. Mannion, *Postmodern ecclesiologies*, 129.

1.3.3.2. Church

The term 'church' has already been explained as the tangible community where Christians congregate for worship, prayer, sharing, instruction, contemplation and mission. Here the following questions are asked, 'what is the church?' and 'where is the church?' In answering these questions the essence and form of the church, the former describing that which is the indispensable qualities of the church while the latter refers to the configuration of the church. Asking the question 'what is the church?' and/or 'where is the church?' involves asking 'what is the essence of church?' and 'what is the (historical) form of church?'

The essence of the church is expressed, by means of the unchanging or permanent factors, throughout its changing historical forms which—from an eschatological approach to ecclesiology—is the people of God as the one and only dwelling-place of God which occurs through the Holy Spirit. While the form of the church is understood by means of the changing and reformable factors of the church and images of the church throughout the church's history. The image(s) of church—as theological expressions—vary with the varying forms of the 'real Church'. The real church refers to the church "as it exists in our world, and in human history."[32] In answering 'where is the church?', McKnight writes that it is "wherever and whenever the people of God is the dwelling-place of God in Christ through the Spirit."[33] The dwelling-place of God is where the gospel of Christ is "preached, taught, embodied and used as a guide", which is otherwise known as the *regula fidei*. McKnight notes that *regula fidei* can "mark where the church is." From this eschatological perspective, McKnight explains that the marks of the church function at a specific level when local churches practice *regula fidei*: when local churches endeavour to be the one, holy, catholic and apostolic church as well as, instead of seeing themselves as 'autonomous and disconnected from all other churches', endeavouring to connect with the 'great tradition of the church in all its forms and in the world at large'. The cause of illuminating such an endeavour of the local church is that the church, as 'one', in its current condition has been torn apart by certain differences—for example the Reformation.

However by reciting the creedal line of 'one, holy, catholic and apostolic church' in the Nicene Creed, the local church through faith is declaring

---

32. Küng, *The church*, 5.
33. McKnight, *Ecclesiology*, 450.

'here is the church'. Such a perspective denotes the concepts of ecumenical inclusivity and exclusivity in 'being church': how to 'be' church in dealing with the complexities of diversity and otherness today.

1.3.3.3. Marks of the church and the nature of these marks

As a line in the Nicene Creed suggests, the four marks of the church are: 'one, holy, catholic and apostolic church'. Each one of these marks is an isolated, albeit integrated, adjective or attribute, hence there are four marks of the church. They are made by faith and should be made in faith to avoid losing their meaning as integrated components, which cannot be detached from their context, of the triune God. Moltmann suggests that acknowledging the one, holy, catholic and apostolic church is also an acknowledgement of the lordship of Christ as "uniting, sanctifying, comprehensive and commissioning."[34] Each of these components, and the associated mark of the church, can be seen as statements of faith, hope, and action.

The first mark of 'one church', with its associated component 'uniting', is accompanied by a statement of faith to unite Christ with all church members; a statement of hope that identifies the ideal of the unity of God's people and the unity of all mankind; and a statement of action that declares that the church ought to be one. The second mark of the church, albeit only in terms of the Nicene Creed and not importance, is a Holy church. The associated component is 'sanctifying' and is a statement of faith in that it denotes the holiness of Christ who acts on all sinners. As a statement of hope the holy and sanctifying church understands holiness as a prophetic promise of the coming divine glory; and as a statement of action the church should fight sin and sanctify its righteousness. The third mark of the church, again only it is credal order, is a Catholic Church with its integrated component of being comprehensive. This translates into a statement of faith that acknowledges the limitless lordship of Christ; a statement of hope that denotes partaking of the catholicity of the coming kingdom; and a statement of action that includes testifying everywhere to the all-embracing kingdom. The final mark of the church is 'apostolic', which as a component is 'commissioning'. This translates into a statement of faith that accepts the mission of Christ and the Spirit; a statement of hope that acknowledges belonging to the beginning of the messianic era; and a statement of action that includes the one people of the one church laying the

---

34. Moltmann, *The church in the power of the spirit*, 338.

foundations of unity among men. This should be considered as a summary of the characteristics of the marks of the church. Therefore, further insight should be given of the four marks and their characteristic dimensions.

Firstly, the nature of the marks of the church as statements of faith denote that the church acknowledges its existence as a result of Christ's actions, thus acknowledging that the marks of the church as characteristics are, first and foremost, the activity of Christ. In other words, faithfully stating the activity of Christ in and with the church and its members. Secondly, the nature of the marks of the church as statements of hope denote that the church's existence is rooted in Christ's messianic mission, therefore its marks—or characteristics—are messianic predicates. Thirdly, the nature of the marks of the church as statements of action denote that there is a course for action in response to these characteristics as statements of faith and hope. Moltmann explains that their characteristics bear the essential nature, or essence, of the church therefore faith, hope and action "are the genesis of the form of the church visible to the world in unity, holiness, catholicity and apostolicity."[35] In other words, the church lives dynamically, throughout historical form, in the 'one, holy, catholic and apostolic' rule of Christ visible through faith, hope and action.

1.3.3.4. Unity

In accordance with the concept of 'one' church, as characterised by the marks of the church, the theoretical action of the church is that it ought to be one, which creates a tension as the church has been ripped apart by certain differences. This is immediately apparent by the reality of the many churches today, thus there is a tension between unity of the 'one' church and diversity of the plurality of churches. There are over 200 churches that belong to the World Council of Churches alone, which is quite apart from the Roman Catholic Church and some Protestant churches that do not want to take part in the World Council. In observing the plurality of churches as incorporated into the 'one' church, four approaches have been developed which allow such an observation. Firstly, an imperalist approach that declares there is only one observable (or empirical) church, and it should be known and treated as the true church. Secondly, a Platonic approach which draws a basic distinction between the empirical church and the ideal church. Thirdly, an eschatological approach suggesting that the

---

35. Moltmann, *The church in the power of the spirit*, 340.

current disunity of the church will be eradicated on the last day. Lastly, a biological approach which draws comparison between the historical evolution of the church and the growing of branches on a tree.

The first approach, referred to as the imperialist approach, maintained by the Roman Catholic Church prior to the Second Vatican Council, declares that there is only one true church and that all others are frauds, pretenders, or resemblances of the real thing. The second approach, as illustrated in the excerpt above, has gained little support in mainstream Theology. Although, some scholars have suggested that a distinction may lie between the 'visible' and 'invisible' church. The third approach, which is eschatological, lies in the understanding of the distinctions between the visible and invisible church and denotes that the present situation of disunity will be abolished on the last day. The last approach referred to as a biological approach, denotes an image of the church similar to that of a tree and its branches. Such an approach allows for the different churches to be understood as having an organic unity, despite being institutionally different.

What can be noticed throughout these four approaches is that the church already possesses an element of unity through its 'common calling from God', Ignatius of Antioch's disposition that the unity of the church lies in Christ as well as Küng's distinction that the unity of the church is grounded in the saving work of God in Christ. Therefore 'unity' should be understood theologically, not sociologically and not organisationally. In understanding the 'unity' of the church theologically it is imperative to draw on theories from scholars of ecclesiology. Küng and Moltmann's discussions on the phenomenon of 'unity' of the church are therefore used for their theological discourse on the topic. As a point of departure, both Küng and Moltmann acknowledge that there are a plurality of churches that ought to be united, in diversity, as one church.[36] Küng discusses that the unity of the church presupposes a multiplicity of local churches, regional churches and different types of churches and that these various churches need not deny their origins; situations; languages; history; customs; traditions and way of life and thought that differentiate them from other churches in order to be united as one church. Furthermore, in unity, said multiplicity of churches should recognise one another as legitimate therefore being 'one' church with no objections to one another's diversity. Similarly, Moltmann illustrates that churches, as communities, that are divided by time and

36. Küng, *The church*, 269–76; Moltmann, *The church in the power of the spirit*, 343.

space "recognise one another through their identity in Christ and the common Spirit", recognising one another as members of the 'one' church.[37] As such, churches co-exist, in unity, with their various diversities, which can be jeopardised when co-existence becomes confrontational when differences are excluding and/or exclusive.

In closing this theoretical section on the relative aspects of ecclesiology, the tensions, and theories thereof, between unity and diversity as well as that between identity and otherness are considered in order to gain insights and perspectives that assisted in developing a theory for praxis. Such insights, especially into the tension between identity and otherness, aided notably when asking 'what ought to be going on?'—a question that is associated with Osmer's so-called normative task of practical theological interpretation. Therefore this theoretical outline serves as the introduction, or basis, of discussions that occur in later chapters.

---

37. Moltmann, *The church in the power of the spirit*, 343.

Chapter 2

CHURCHES IN PLURALITY

THE PROPOSED RESEARCH PLAN was to find three churches, within one metropolitan or city. This was duly achieved. Below is an explanation on why this plan was proposed, the importance of sharing such information stresses the importance of describing everything when entering the field of research. The reason for giving the explanation, immediately below, is not so that one can simply gain a geographical understanding of the locations where the research was conducted. It is rather due to the geography forming the outer layer of the layered contexts that the ritual-liturgical data is embedded in as well as illustrating the relative aspects that influence 'being church'.

2.1. THE CITY OF CENTURION

Centurion is an ever growing city, situated between Pretoria and Johannesburg, in Gauteng, Republic of South Africa. Centurion, previously known as Verwoerdburg (or *Verwoerdburg Stad*), falls into the City of Tshwane - the same municipality as Pretoria. The City originates from the Lyttelton Township that was marked out on a farm named *Droogegrond* in 1904. In 1964, it was given its City Council status under the name of Lyttelton, combining the aforementioned township with that of Irene and *Doornkloof*. Four years later, Lyttelton changed to Verwoerdburg after the assassination of former South African Prime Minister Hendrick Verwoerd. Verwoerdburg was changed to Centurion on 28 of June 1995. Today, Centurion is made up of many more suburbs (or townships) than the ones mentioned above. There is constant expansion and development as the population increases as a result of urbanisation.

The City of Centurion has been in existence for many decades, there are areas and suburbs that have been inhabited since the city's foundation on the one hand. While on the other hand, there are new areas and suburbs that are being established regularly. The latest census information states that there are just short of 250,000 residents in Centurion.

Pretoria, to the north of Centurion, serves as the administrative capital of the Republic of South Africa. It is home to the Union Buildings, the South African Reserve Bank as well as an abundance of embassies. Johannesburg, approximately seventy-five kilometres south of Pretoria, sees itself as the business or financial metropolis of the country. It boasts with Sandton City being the richest square mile in Africa and is home to the Johannesburg Stock Exchange (JSE). With the respective statuses that these cities boast, Pretoria and Johannesburg appeal to millions upon millions of people. Not only within the borders of South Africa but also from other African countries and even further abroad. As proof of the above, Gauteng shows the highest percentage of non-South African citizens in the country with 7,2 percent of the province's population consisting of foreign nationals.

Gauteng is the smallest of the nine provinces of the Republic of South Africa at just over 18,000 square kilometres—1,8 percent of the countries land area, yet it has the highest number of the country's population living within its borders—with over twelve million people. KwaZulu-Natal, by comparison, has a population of just over ten million people, occupying 7,7 percent of the countries land area.

The attraction being what it is, draws a multiplicity of people from different cultures, races and religious beliefs. Without relying too much on statistics, the population increase between the 2006 census and last census conducted in 2011 meant that Gauteng overtook KwaZulu-Natal as the province with the highest population. Some of that increase is due to lives being added to the population in the form of child birth, it cannot make up the entire increase on its own. Therefore it can be rationalised that a significant amount of the addition to the population is as a result of both immigration from other South African provinces and from other countries. Due to the fact that South Africa is so culturally and linguistically diverse it is reasonable to claim that, ignoring the international additions to the population, some more cultures and religious beliefs have been added to the equation than those that call themselves locals. Adding to this is more races of people that are immigrating to Gauteng from other countries around the world, such as the Middle Eastern and Far Eastern countries, which also add to the number of cultures and religions.

One of the reasons for choosing Centurion is because it showed a proportional mixture of new and old. There are townships and/or suburbs that were established fifty years ago or more and then there are areas that were developed more recently, that are finding room to expand to this day. Another reason is that with any city comes a large array of cultures, in Gauteng there are three cities within a hundred kilometres of each other. There is massive national and international interest in all three cities, as explained above each city has its attractions as individuals—as three cities combined they may prove irresistible for people seeking a change in career and/or location.

It was one of the objectives to conduct the research at three churches with different liturgical traditions. A mainline congregation was found in the form of, what will be called, Hennops Methodist Church. A higher liturgical congregation was found in the form of Smuts Anglican Church, a pseudonym for the sake of anonymity. Titans Church, also a pseudonym, serves as a charismatic church. It should be noted that the liturgical traditions of these churches are not as strict as their titles or typologies depict, the concept of bricolage should be considered. The Anglican church in question sticks rather strictly to an organ and choir, whilst the Methodist church flows in between the more traditional organ and the more modernly acceptable worship band which includes the use of electronic instruments as well as a set of drums. The definitions, therefore are well formed guidelines and not concrete parameters to which the church and it congregants must conform.

Semi-structured interviews were conducted at all three of these churches, after permission was granted by the authorities, or leadership, at each of the churches. The churches also gave permission for their services to be observed and recorded (audio only) and for notes in the form of 'thick descriptions' to be taken. These three churches, as well as the suburbs that they are in, were chosen because of their similarities, for example they are all in a similar financial bracket—none of the areas are associated with so-called 'lower-class' or poor and none of them are havens for the super wealthy. They also have their differences, besides their liturgical traditions, two of the churches are much closer together in terms of distance than the third one is, the two that are nearer each other are also in suburbs that have a longer history than the third church.

A brief description of how the above situation came to be will be given on each church. These churches were chosen for a few reasons. Firstly because they all fall within the Centurion city limits and are within suburbs of the city. Secondly, each of the three churches is in a well developed suburb and each has expanding suburbs surround it. All three of the churches, and their suburbs, have a recognisable cultural diversity and similar income statuses. The suburbs in which these churches are situated each have the ability to function independently, that is each suburb here has its own schools, shopping areas and churches.

Furthermore, all three churches use English as a medium of communication. Their services and any other communication with the congregation or members is done in English. This being stated, not all the worshippers at any of the three churches will claim English as being their mother tongue. Therefore not all the worshippers at any of the churches will conform outright to 'English culture', instead they will have their own cultural backgrounds that are not entirely the same as the church which they attend. All the official languages of the Republic of South Africa are represented in the city of Centurion with Afrikaans being the most popular home language, spoken by slightly more than fifty percent (50,56percent) of the population in Centurion. English is the home language to 26,59percent of the population followed by: Sepedi which is the home language of just over five percent (5,35percent) of the Centurion population; Setswana (3,83percent); isiZulu (3,35percent); Sesotho (2,92percent); isiXhosa (2,68percent); Xitsonga (1,46percent); isiNdebele (1,34percent); Tshivenda (1,29percent); SiSwati (0,45percent) and Sign Language which is the home language to four-hundred and sixteen people in Centurion (0,18percent).

In the case of all three of the churches the minister(s), priest(s) or pastor(s) was/were contacted and an appointment was requested. During the appointment, the research aims were communicated to the relevant party as well as what would be requested of the church and its congregation. While in the appointment, certain aspects of the church and its liturgy were brought to light and questioned in able to ensure that they fell into the correct categories, namely: a higher liturgical congregation; a mainline congregation and a charismatic church. During each appointment it was requested that the contact person would check with the relevant parties to ensure that the research would not meet any opposition whilst being conducted at the church(es). In each case, the contact person at the church responded positively after checking with their relevant parties and the research was given approval. Finally, an informed consent was given to each of the churches in order to ensure that each church and its managerial role-players were correctly informed before consent—either verbal or written—was given.

Below is a description of each of the churches, briefly giving an idea of each church, its establishment, membership size and number of worship services per week. All the information below, which was gathered by means of following a systematic process, was discovered either in conversation with the relevant priests/pastors/reverends or via email with these same individuals. In some instances the priests/pastors/reverends were unable to provide the information and either contacted administrative people at the church directly or suggested it be done as they keep records of the all the information that was requested.

The idea behind gaining this information was to provide a full, informed, picture of the churches; their history and their congregations. Thus within their layered contexts, which is also the layered contexts in these congregations in which the ritual of prayer is performed. This is referred to as exegeting the congregation because the congregation may be considered a culture; and it provides a description of 'being church' or *lex (con) vivendi*. In her chapter 'Exegeting the congregation', Tisdale makes comparisons throughout to anthropologists and ethnographers and how they have tools and guides for gaining knowledge of new cultures and societies. According to Tisdale, there are seven symbols of "congregational life" that provide information for congregational exegesis, they are: "history and archival materials", "demographics", "stories and guided interviews", "ritual and liturgical patterns", "church architecture and the visual arts", "people" and "congregational events and activities."[1] Each of these help develop the full, informed picture of each church and their congregations that are being studied. Hence certain requests were made to the relevant parties to obtain and ascertain information that related to developing the embedding of the ritual data in its layered context. Certain aspects of the above mentioned list were handled by the research conducted through semi structured interviews and by observing the worship services. Other aspects such as the "history and archival materials" and the demographics were requested

---

1. Tisdale, *Teaching Preaching as a Christian Practice*, 83.

from the churches' offices as mentioned above. Below is an informational brief of each church that was part the research process.

2.1.1. "Hennops Methodist"

This Methodist church was planted in the 1970's and is situated in one of the more developed (or older) areas of Centurion. There are approximately 32,155 people that reside in the surrounding suburbs. The church has a membership of around 2,000 people. A regular Sunday will see about 650 people join in worship over three different services. There are two morning services, one after the other, and a third service in the evening.

The first service on a Sunday morning is targeted at people around the age of 55 and above, and is generally attended by pensioners aged 65 and older. The second of the morning services is targeted at people over the age of 30, while the average age of people in attendance is closer to 50 years old. The evening service is designed for the younger members and targeted at people 15 years and older. However the average age of people at this service is about 30 years old. All three services are conducted in English, most often by one of the ordained ministers on staff. This information was provided by one of the ministers and is according to the church's records.

2.1.2. "Titans Church"

Titans Church is a relatively small congregation on the edge of one of the oldest suburbs of Centurion. However the edge of this suburb is met by a newer and developing suburb that features modern apartment blocks and townhouses. There are nearly 50,000 people residing in and around the suburb in which Titans Church is located.

The church was planted in the late 1990's and has two pastors on staff. The church building is quaint and fractionally smaller than a school hall, there is a membership of two hundred people. Titans Church has two worship services on a Sunday and has between eighty and one hundred worshippers at each session. The second service is a carbon copy of the first service with: the same worship set, same sermon and the same target group. The average age of these worship services is approximately thirty-five years old, children from the age of seven years old and up attend kids' ministry, which is held in the adjacent building. This data was provided by one of the pastors at the church in response to the following questions:

1. When was the church planted?
2. How many pastors are on staff?
3. What is the membership size of the church?
4. What is the average amount of worshippers in each service?
5. What is the average age of worshippers in each service?

2.1.3. "Smuts Anglican"

Smuts Anglican, similarly to Titans Church, is a relatively small congregation. The church is located in an area of Centurion that has a rich history dating back to the early 20th Century. This historic area and its surrounding suburbs are home to more than 18,370 people. The church is approximately the same size as Titans Church, and while an accurate estimate of the membership cannot be given, the average attendance of the first worship service in the morning is approximately one-hundred worshippers. The average age, as a calculated approximation is probably similar to that of the first worship service on a Sunday at Hennops Methodist—around sixty years of age.

2.2. CHURCHES IN THE MIDST OF PLURALITY

This critical section is a description in response to the general question of the descriptive-empirical task: 'what is going on?' In this context there are two parts to this question. The first part of the question is 'what is going on in the worship service(s)?' This will be answered first by means of describing what was observed by means of thick descriptions. The necessity of doing this is to describe the form and content of prayers they are able to be studied, which should lead to examples of *lex orandi* and *lex credendi*. The second part of the question is 'what is going on with the worshippers at the church(es)?', this question will be answered by means of describing what was shared in the interviews.

The data below is that which describes 'what is going on', by means of categorisations, in the worship services—from the participatory observations as well as the opinion of the worshipper come interviewee. In other words, the data described and discussed below are examples of 'what is going on' in terms of the three separated aspects of the aphorism of *lex orandi, lex credendi, lex (con)vivendi*. The aim here is to describe a narrative of three churches in one pluralistic city, told as it was observed and as it is experienced by those that attend one of the churches for worship. The descriptions that will follow have been placed into subsections. There are three subsections, one for each of the churches. After the descriptions are shared below, there will be space for the relevant similarities, differences and other noteworthy episodes, situations or contexts to be discussed.

2.2.1. What is Going on in the Worship Services at Smuts Anglican

The first part of the description of what is going on at Smuts Anglican is the noticeable similarities across the three worship services that were observed through participation. The latter part of the description will be a guide through the important events, situations or contexts that were observed at each, individual worship service.

Smuts Anglican, as the pseudonym suggests, is an Anglican church, it therefore fits into the category of a higher liturgical congregation. The most obvious observation is the strict obedience to the order of service, in this case "The Holy Eucharist." This was found after examination of the observations, followed by a search for specific prayers that were prayed during the worship services, culminating in the finding of the above mentioned order of service being found in An Anglican Prayer Book. The order of service is fixed, leaving minimal room for adjustments, however the clergy manage to make the service feel more casual than the order of service insinuates. In the three services that were observed, "The Holy Eucharist" order of service was used with subtle variances from service to service.

Once the order of service was followed to completion, the remainder of the service was informal to the point where it came across as a social, inclusive, gathering. During the times after the completion of "The Holy Eucharist", the informal events such as: singing happy birthday to members of the congregation, the blessing of a birthday cake or greeting guests and hearing their testimonies or the introductions of themselves to the congregation. In the mood of being informal, it was observed that there was no strict time to finish the service neither the worshippers nor the clergy seemed in a rush to finish the service.

Overall, it seemed as if the order of service that is used was well rehearsed. It came across from the observations as seamless and the clergy to avoid it being boring, dreary or mundane. The worshippers seemed completely absorbed in the worship service and its liturgical rituals. The worshippers at Smuts Anglican appeared to be comfortable and content with the amount of movement during the worship service. There were times where the congregation stood for ten minutes at a time, sometimes in silence while they wait for the clergy to guide them through certain items that are part of the order of service. Throughout the service there were many occasions where the worshippers transitioned from sitting, to standing, back to sitting and then kneeling. They were requested by the clergy to stand or be seated and usually when an announcement of "let us pray" is made, a substantial amount of the congregation would either drop to one knee or kneel completely.

As mentioned above, the following of the order of service is strict and fixed. In addition to this there was little to no sense of bricolage. The church makes use of less modern instruments, sticking to an organ, piano and a choir. There are no guitars, electric nor acoustic, and no drums. In terms of technology, Smuts Anglican makes no use of data projectors. All the hymns and songs of fellowship are found in books that are in the rails on the back of the pews, instead of them being projected, at the front of the church, on a large screen. In terms of the prayers in each of the three services, the majority involved responses from the congregation. The prayers in the worship services were mostly read, by the clergy, from 'The Holy Eucharist' in 'An Anglican Prayer Book'. In some instances the congregation responded and in others the congregation read certain parts of the prayer with the clergy. The prayers that were said from the prayer book use specific terminology. This should be discussed and interpreted in the proceeding chapters. Along with the terminology, there is a methodological process that flows throughout the worship service which is echoed through prayers that are used. This should also be discussed and interpreted at a later stage, in the chapters that follow.

Overall, it can be said that the tradition of the church is dominant throughout the worship service. However where there is tradition, on one end of the proverbial candle, then there should be culture on the other end. This poses the question: where do tradition (church) and culture meet? This too will be discussed through interpretation in the next chapter as well as the one after that which will focus more on a normative approach.

Lastly, at the end of the services when the notices for the week were announced to the congregation, there was one notice that stood out. This was the announcement that anyone in need of prayer should go to the rails, before the altar, after the service where they would be met with someone that will pray with or for them. Thus another question is posed: why is this offered? There are multiple reasons why such an opportunity would be made available. An overall description of what is going on during the worship service, in general, has been provided above. This has left some unanswered questions, that will be answered at later stages throughout. The next step is to provide descriptive-empirical data on what is going on in the worship services individually. This process involves detailing specific events, situations or contexts that happened at each of the worship services.

The aim of this narrative is simply to describe detailed empirical data. Therefore, there will be questions asked without indulging deeply into the interpretative, this will be done thoroughly in the next chapter. With this in mind, descriptions of the services, individually, will be given below.

2.2.1.1. First Observation at Smuts Anglican

The first service that was observed and participated in marked the third Sunday of lent. On the Anglican liturgical calendar, the third Sunday of lent bears the theme 'repent or you shall perish'. This theme is strongly and clearly put across, its wording is observed as a warning. Before a single word was said by the clergy, the church bells were rung four minutes before the service started. This came across as significantly traditional, the bells announcing the imminent commencing of the worship service. Before, and during, the ringing of the bells there was little to no conversation taking place among the worshippers that were waiting in the church. An atmosphere of reverence and respect was being upheld by the worshippers. For the most part, the worshippers share slight nods or smiles as a form of greeting fellow worshippers.

The worship service was opened in the form of a prayer, said by the priest. Included in the prayer was a brief prayer for the protection and guidance of the children, shortly after which they were instructed to leave the church for children's church (Sunday school). The priest had the responsibility of introducing the theme, after which he said to the congregation: "May the Lord be with you", the congregation responded to this by saying: "And also with you." In light of this worship service recognising the period of lent, the ten commandments are read by one of the clergy on duty. After each commandment was read, the congregation responded by saying: "Amen, Lord have mercy."

The next item on the agenda was confession. The clergy allowed the worshippers to pray and in doing so confessing their sins from the comfort of their pews. After allowing the worshippers time to confess, the same member of the clergy closed this period of confession with a prayer. Following the confession was 'the collect', the priest prayed and then announced the prayer for 'the collect'. This prayer was prayed by the entire congregation and clergy. They prayed as one voice, out loud.

What proceeded 'the collect', and prayer thereof, were the readings. There was one reading from the Old Testament, followed by the reading of a Psalm and then a reading from the New Testament. Behind the altar, against the foremost wall of the church is a large wooden cross. Before each reading, which was announced by the 'synaxis', the reader walked to face the cross; bowed before it - with his or her back to the congregation and then proceeded to the lectern to read the relevant scripture. At the end of each reading, the reader concluded with a brief statement: for the Old Testament reading the reader proclaimed "Hear the word of the Lord" to which the worshippers respond with "Thanks be to God." For the reading of the Psalm, the proclamation and response were the same. To conclude the reading from the New Testament, the reader proclaimed "This is the Gospel of Christ", the worshippers responded by saying: "Praise be to our Lord." Once the readings were completed, the steward—who read the New Testament reading—announced the reading of the Nicene Creed. As one voice, the worshippers chanted their way through the creed in a monotone fashion. Many of the worshippers recited the Nicene Creed from memory, others followed along in one of the books from the rails attached to the pews in front of them.

All the events above had taken up the first twenty-five minutes of the worship service. The priest had readied himself to deliver his sermon. During the sermon, the priest made modern comparisons to the readings that were delivered earlier. As an example of this, when preaching about the parable consisting of being invited to a banquet, the priest explained being invited via email. The priest also makes modern references to the likes of online shopping and Internet banking.

In terms of how God was perceived throughout this sermon, the priest constantly referred to 'God as a provider'. The sermon was concluded when the priest said to the worshippers "May God bless you", the worshippers respond with a simple 'amen'. Following the sermon, the 'synaxis' who had a book in front of him places one knee on the ground and began to pray.

The book seemed to contain a list of topics that must be prayed about, there were many topics that were covered in this prayer including praying for specific people and their situations. When the 'synaxis' was praying for specific people, their names and even their circumstances were mentioned on a few occasions. Some topics of this prayer were broad and general, such as praying for the political situations in South Africa. Other topics, such as the examples alluded to above were more specific and detailed. As the prayer began, most of the worshippers in the congregation went down on one knee—other worshippers were kneeling completely.

On conclusion of the prayer, the entire congregation of worshippers stood for 'the peace'. The worshippers began to greet those around, typically starting with those next to them - in the same pew and then turning to those in front of and behind them. Each person that was greeted, is met with the phrase "peace be with you", usually provoking a response of "and also with you." During 'the peace', the musicians and choir sang a hymn, the clergy descended from the altar. Each of them walked among the pews, greeting each and every worshipper in attendance. They, too, greeted the worshippers with the phrase "peace be with you" while shaking the worshippers' hands or giving them a hug. At some points, the priest and members of the clergy paused to have brief conversations with some of the worshippers they were greeting. The pauses that they made to chat and ask questions about the wellbeing of a worshipper or their absent loved ones conveyed a great sense of fellowship and community. During 'the peace', while the congregation stood and waited their turn to be greeted by the priest, the collection was taken. Every single worshipper had remained standing since the announcement of 'the peace'.

The next major liturgical ritual on the agenda for the worship service, was the Eucharist. The priest, on his return to the altar, announced and then prayed 'the fourth Eucharist prayer'. The priest suggested "let us pray", at this point the worshippers either took their seats or kneeled with one or both knees. They remained in their various positions while the priest and other clergy blessed the elements. After each element is blessed, a small handheld bell was rung. When the bell was rung the clergy surrounding the table hastily took a knee and then returned to a standing position.

The final ritual act, before the congregation could partake in receiving the Eucharist, was a murmuring of The Lord's Prayer. The entire liturgical ritual process, from the praying of 'the fourth Eucharist prayer' to the completion of The Lord's prayer took longer than ten minutes to perform.

The congregation could then go forward to the rails at the altar and receive the Eucharist. The orderly fashion in which this was done started with the choir and musicians going forward first. Once they had returned to their pews and instruments, the door steward stood in line with the foremost pew. As he moved backwards, those in front of him left their pews, walked to the rails, kneeled, received the Eucharist and returned to their pews. The door steward slowly walked backwards, along those in front of him to go up and receive the Eucharist, until he reached the back of the church—where the choir is situated.

After the choir and musicians returned to their places, the choir leader announced the songs of fellowship that were to be sung while the worshippers partake in receiving the Eucharist. The choir leader invited the worshippers to join the choir in singing these songs of fellowship. As the worshippers returned to their seats from the rails at the altar, some sat and bowed their heads while others kneeled. Each worshipper took their time after receiving to silently pray by themselves—some for a much longer time than others. Once all the worshippers inside the church had received the Eucharist and returned to their pews, the children were then led in by the adults that supervise them. They stayed in a single file line, slowly walked up to the rails and received the Eucharist. Once they had consumed the elements, they turned from the rails and led back out of the church. It was observed that each worshipper, on completing their time of prayer after receiving the Eucharist, made the sign of the cross. The priest and the clergy on duty only received the Eucharist once the worshippers, adults and children, had received. Once they have received, they wiped the goblets and placed a cloth over the elements that remained on the table.

The priest took a moment to thank the choir for the music before announcing that the church would now give thanks. This was done in the form of a prayer, from the prayer book. One of the stewards then took to the lectern to read the announcements for the week. Something that was particularly unique about this worship service, was the resignation of the church administrator. The priest announced that he and other worshippers, that he had invited forward, would pray for the resigning church administrator. Below is the transcription:

First person prays: "Thank you for the blessing that [Administrator] has been to us over the last fourteen years. The ways in which [he/she] has blessed us with [his/her] gifts and the ways in which you have called [him/

her] and grown [him/her] and prepared [him/her] for this ministry. We thank you for [him/her] . . . [inaudible] . . . in Jesus name."

Congregation responds: "Amen."

Second person prays: "Lord Jesus, we thank you for [Administrator]. We pray for her guidance in the future in the new job . . . [inaudible muttering] . . . We thank you Jesus, Amen."

Congregation responds: "Amen."

Third person prays: "Dear Lord, we thank you for [Administrator]. Thank you for fourteen years of service [he/she] has given Smuts Anglican. And we thank you as well for [his/her] ongoing service to Smuts Anglican and this parish. We wish [him/her] all the very best . . . "

Fourth person prays: " . . . [inaudible] . . . courage, strength, perseverance . . . [inaudible whispering] . . . amen."

Congregation responds: "Amen."

The worship service had now become more casual, as the liturgy had been completed. The priest announced some visitors to the parish, that he was aware of. The priest also asked for any other visitors to announce themselves, he casually walked through the congregation while doing so. He approached the visitors, greeted them and offered them the opportunity to introduce themselves or share anything that they wished to share. Another situation that was unique to this worship service, was that members of the congregation had made a request to the priest for the church to sing 'happy birthday' to one of the children in the church. The priest duly allowed this.

Before the priest closed the service, he announced "Let us pray for Africa", the worshippers and clergy recited the 'Prayer for Africa'. The priest then closed the service by saying to the worshippers: "Go in peace and serve the Lord." The worshippers responded with a simple 'amen'. A closing hymn was then announced, at which point the congregation stood as the clergy gathered in a formation, leaving the altar and proceeding out of the church. The singing of the closing hymn was loud, there was no awkward humming or mumbling sounds. There were some worshippers that prayed quietly and quickly, after the closing hymn, before taking to their feet and leaving the church. The choir continued to sing as the worshippers led out of the church.

2.2.1.2. Second Observation at Smuts Anglican

The second observation done at Smuts Anglican was on the second Sunday after Easter. The first observation was during the period of lent. It was observed that the layout and decorations inside the church had not changed since the first observation, leading to the assumption that there was no different, specific layout or decoration for the lent and Easter period.

The worship service began with the worshippers joining in with the choir and enjoying songs of fellowship. While observing the singing, it was noticed that the church was considerably fuller than it was at the last observed worship service. After the songs of fellowship were completed, temporarily, there was a reciprocal prayer from the Anglican prayer book—from which the liturgy is taken, namely :"The Holy Communion":

All: "Almighty God to whom all hearts are open all desires known and from whom no secrets are hid: cleanse the thoughts of our hearts by the inspiration of your Holy Spirit that we may perfectly love you and worthily magnify your holy Name; through Christ our Lord.

Prayer leader: "Lord, have mercy."
Congregation: "Lord, have mercy."
Prayer leader: "Christ, have mercy."
Congregation: "Christ, have mercy."
Prayer leader: "Lord, have mercy."
Congregation: "Lord, have mercy."

During the prayer, all the worshippers in proximity had their heads bowed and their eyes closed—even when a member of the clergy is praying from the altar. Proceeding the prayer was 'the collect' for the second Sunday after Easter. At this point there was a small amount of laughter and humour due to the confusion surrounding whether the worshippers should be seated or standing. While on a more informal event, it was about fifteen minutes since the worship service began and there were worshippers arriving and entering the church. Thus it seemed there was no fuss made over late-comers from other worshippers, clergy or the worshippers arriving. These new arrivals found a vacant space on a pew. They slowly found their way towards the front of the church due to the church, seemingly, having filled up with worshippers from the back of the church as its pews were crammed full of worshippers. On the contrary, there was considerably more space, or vacant seats, at the pews towards the front of the church.

Following 'the collect', there was the Old Testament and Psalm reading. The relevant readings were read by a worshipper from the congregation—this was not the case at the last observation. The readings in the previous observation were read by the clergy on duty. The prayer, that was read from the Psalms, was read in a monotone fashion by all the worshippers. Some of the worshippers followed along in the Bibles that are provided in the pew rails. As noted above, there was a miscommunication earlier that concluded with providing humour among the worshippers and clergy. There was a second miscommunication made by one of the clergy to the worshippers, however it was promptly corrected by the organist. The organist was also the choir leader, the correction was made as the worshippers were standing up to join in song.

During the singing of the hymn, there was no mumbling along from the worshippers. The majority of worshippers sang with vigour and some display of emotion. There was no dull drone that can be associated with more aged hymns. This hymn was followed by the New Testament reading and as it was read the worshippers responded with "Praise Jesus." The worshippers were still standing, since the beginning of the hymn, while the reader continued with the reading. Many of the worshippers were following along with the reader, in the Bibles provided in the pew rails and chair bags. The reading ended with the worshippers proclaiming "Praise be to Christ our Lord." The next liturgical ritual was the chanting of the Nicene Creed, which was done in a poetic rhythm yet a monotone fashion—recited by the worshippers and clergy alike.

The sermon preached at this worship service was preached by one of the lay clergy and not the priest, even though he was on duty and seated behind the lectern. The preacher is a lady, who was soft spoken and preached delicately. She appeared calm and revered as she spoke to the worshippers instead of 'lecturing' at them. It was observed that she preached as if she had practised her sermon over and over again, she did well to keep eye contact with the worshippers—seldom reading from her notes. Following the sermon was a call to prayer, a moment was made to the worshippers that allowed them to assume their various, preferred, praying stances. The 'synaxis' began the prayer, the first part of which was in line with the sermon that was preached. The second part of the prayer was a prayer for Jesus to enter "our homes." The third part of the prayer was that "we" would count in His numbers. Forth, was a prayer for a time of praise. The fifth part of the prayer, was broad and was a prayer for the blessing and direction of South Africa's political leaders. The final part of the prayer was a communal prayer, which was reciprocal—where the worshippers responded to what was being prayed for by the 'synaxis'. This served as the closure of the prayer. At the end of each of the parts of the prayer, mentioned above, was a response from the worshippers. Their responses, however, were not as in unison or rhythm as was the case earlier in the worship service.

Another prayer followed the prayer that has just ended. This prayer was a prayer for peace and was prayed before 'the peace'. Immediately after the prayer, the worshippers began to turn and greet those around them with "Peace be with you", responded with—as was the case in the last observation—"and also with you" by each the worshippers that was greeted. Again, in repetition of the previous Sunday, the priest and the lay preacher descended from the altar and walked through each pew, greeting each and every worshipper as they went. They shook hands with each person and uttered the phrase: "Peace be with you." In response, the worshipper muttered back: "And also with you." Throughout the duration of this process, the worshippers—led by the choir—sang hymns and songs of fellowship. Their shared voice was loud, clear and pleasing to listen to. There was emotion involved in their singing. The vigour of the singing was aided by the sizeable choir, that led the way.

Once this ritual was completed, the worshippers stood waiting in silence for the next instruction as the clergy prepared the table for the Eucharist. The blessing of the elements was done in prayer by the lay preacher, whose sermon was heard earlier, the worshippers responded to certain parts of the prayer. Proceeding this, the priest read a prayer from a book on the altar. The congregation, typically, responded at the end of each part of the prayer. An instruction was given for the worshippers to join in song, as they did so a few children entered the church—assumedly finding their way to their parents. The worshippers, then seated, prayed once again. The clergy were kneeling in front of the table while the priest blessed the elements and read the last supper narrative. The priest then read another prayer—the worshippers responded at the end of the prayer. The clergy then returned to behind the table, joining the priest, this was followed by the singing of the Lord's prayer. At the last observation, the Lord's prayer was said not sung. Many of the worshippers were kneeling as they sung the Lord's prayer.

There was a massive crescendo as the congregation sung the final lines of the Lord's prayer, this showed and evoked emotion among the worshippers, clergy and choir. Once the singing was completed, another prayer followed and was related to the Eucharist. This was followed by a period of silence. The same worshippers that were kneeling during the singing of the Lord's prayer were still kneeling. As with the first observation, the choir went forward to receive the Eucharist first. However, in the last observation the clergy received last, at this observation they received first while the choir were waiting, kneeling at the rails. Once the choir returned, the foremost pews—full of worshippers—led the way in receiving the Eucharist, followed pew by pew until the back of the church. After receiving the Eucharist, the worshippers made their way—one by one—back to their seats. Once they had returned, they bowed their heads or knelt in a state of prayer or meditation. All the worshippers, whether kneeling or sitting, had their heads bowed. Once the choir and musicians had returned to their pews and instruments respectively, the organist announced and invited the worshippers to join in songs of fellowship. These songs were relative to the Eucharist. The singing continued as the worshippers went forward to receive the Eucharist. While the worshippers were sitting or kneeling in their time of prayer and contemplation, the choir were standing and singing—some with their hands raised while worshipping through songs of fellowship. The choir consisted of ten adults, nine of them were females and there was only one male. Both the organist and pianist were male, they joined the choir in singing while they led the choir by playing their respective instruments.

Once the last worshippers had gone forward and received the Eucharist, the priest invited the children—who were lined up at the door—into the church to partake in the Eucharist. In congruence with the previous observation, the children were lined up in two, single-file lines at the doors of the church and were led in by supervising adults. Each child knelt at the rail, received the Eucharist and walked back out of the church, assumedly returning to their Sunday school classes. The final steps of this ritual process involved the clergy finishing what was left in the cups or silver goblets, after which they rinsed and wiped them. The worshippers waited in silence as the elements of the Eucharist, and their cups and plates, were packed together and covered with a large cloth. There was a reciprocal prayer to conclude the liturgical ritual of the Eucharist.

The priest then called for the announcements to be read, a member of the choir walked up the aisle, to the lectern to read the announcements. A notice that was read, which seemed important to mention in the description: that anyone in need of prayer should come to the rails after the service where they will be met by 'the prayer ministry' after the service.

The worship service was ended with a closing song of fellowship, sung after the priest made a statement to which the worshippers responded.

While the choir and worshippers were singing, the clergy exited the church in a formation. They proceeded to pray hand-in-hand, around a lit candle just outside the door of the church. Once they had concluded their prayer(s), they waited outside to greet each worshipper that led out of the church at the end of the worship service. As the final song ended, the majority of worshippers made their way towards the exit of the church, some worshippers sat and prayed while others knelt before they exited the church. The choir continued to sing, with the aid of the piano and organ, as all the worshippers led slowly out of the church.

2.2.1.3. *Third Observation at Smuts Anglican*

This third and final worship service observation, at Smuts Anglican, began with the entrance of the clergy at nine o'clock. After leading in, and finding their way to their seats around the table, one of the clergy announced the introit hymn. The church is not as full, at the observation, as it was a week prior—at the last observation. After the singing of the introit hymn, the priest requested the worshippers and choir to sing the first two verses again. In opening the service, the priest announced that there were children amongst the worshippers. He said a short prayer for the children before some of them left the church, assumedly for Sunday school. After they left, it was noticed that there were plenty of late-comers. They were in little to no hurry and had minimal concern for causing any interruptions as they made their way to empty spaces in the pews to sit.

This worship service began differently to those previously observed. The priest had taken to the lectern before the liturgy had started, he was speaking about how important the leadership role of the bishop is to the Anglican Church. His need to mention this was due to the upcoming election of a new bishop. From previous observations, the priest normally only addresses the worshippers much later in the worship service. At this point the congregation had been standing for ten minutes. Once the priest was finished with his explanation the 'synaxis' announced the second hymn. There were still families of worshippers arriving and joining in with the worship service at this point, as in they were at least ten minutes late. Already mentioned above the number of worshippers was significantly less than the previous observations, it was noticed that the number of choir members was significantly less than previous occasions as well.

After the second hymn, the 'synaxis' said the familiar phrase: "Let us pray." Automatically, the worshippers sat down—some of them kneeled, as has become the observed norm. This prayer was from the Anglican prayer book. The worshippers read along in what can be described as the usual monotone manner. This was followed by a confessional prayer, this prayer was concluded by the priest and not the 'synaxis'—who initiated the prayer. The worshippers and clergy then follow straight into another short prayer. The 'synaxis', then, kindly asked the worshippers to be seated for the first reading of this worship service, which was taken from the Old Testament. One of the members of the clergy on duty did the reading, this person was one of the clergy that led the priest up to the altar and was seated around the table, at the altar. The reading was ended by the reader saying: "Hear the word of the Lord." To which the congregation responded: "Praise be to God."

The reading was followed by the reading of the Psalm, read by all the worshippers in a monotonous drone. The Psalm that was read was Psalm 27. The 'synaxis' then announced the second reading as well as the person that would read it. This person stepped out from one of the pews, among the worshippers rather than being a member of the clergy, and walked up to the lectern. This reading was done approximately twenty-five minutes into the worship service, at which point there were still worshippers entering the church to join in the worship service. The reader concluded the reading with the phrase: "Praise be to God", to which the worshippers responded, in unison: "Thanks be to God." The 'synaxis' then announced the singing of a third hymn, the worshippers all stood to join the choir in song. The third hymn was followed by the final reading for the worship service, typically from the New Testament - specifically from the Gospel. It was read by one of the lay preachers at the church, who ended the reading with "This is the Gospel of Christ", met by a response from the worshippers.

A liturgical ritual that was unique to this observation, was the 'synaxis'' announcement of the "reconfirming of our faith." This was something that was not experienced in the prior observations. The worshippers read this in a typically monotonous drone that has been associated with other readings and prayers done throughout the worship services that were observed. The liturgical rituals were completed to the point where the priest was given the floor in order to deliver his sermon. He began the sermon by informing the congregation that this Sunday marked the fourth Sunday of Easter and that it is traditionally known as "Shepherd's Sunday." He reminded the worshippers that all of the readings, read before his sermon, gave examples of Jesus as the shepherd—mostly obviously in the reading of Psalm 27. The priest proceeded to explain that shepherds were not counted as part of the community and added that "They are in the periphery."

Another unique aspect was noticed in the form of the priest not preaching from behind the lectern, as is the norm or expectation from prior observations. In this worship service he chose to stroll up and down the aisle while delivering his sermon, with a staff in his hands. The priest, uniquely, asked one of the worshippers to read from John 21:15 and proceeded to explain that he intended to close the sermon with a reading from Revelations 7:9–17. After the sermon, one of the clergy on duty announced the prayer for this morning and shared the page number in the Anglican prayer book, where the worshippers could follow. As the prayer was said, the clergy member was kneeling behind and leaning slightly on a small, low lectern. At the end of each section of this predetermined prayer, the clergy member exclaimed "Lord, hear us." To which the worshippers automatically, and in one voice, responded: "Lord, graciously hear us." This prayer was thorough and many events and situations were prayed for. As the prayer was completed, the worshippers—reading from the Anglican prayer book—prayed as one, closing the prayer. This longer and more specific prayer was followed by 'the peace', which was carried out in its usual manner—as described in the prior observations above. This was met by the announcement of the offertory hymn. While it was being sung, the offering bowls were passed around from worshipper to worshipper whilst being guided from pew to pew by the church wardens. The priest and deacon went around, while the offering was being taken, to each worshipper and wished them "Peace be with you", which was reciprocated by each of the worshippers. While these processes continued, the offertory hymn was completed and the pianist announced the singing of a second hymn while the taking of the offering was completed.

The worshippers stood up before 'the peace' began, they remained standing throughout 'the peace' and the taking of the offering. They remained standing, in prayer, while the elements of the Eucharist were being blessed by the priest. After the blessing of the bread, the 'synaxis' rang a small bell; a candle was raised by another member of the clergy and all around the table kneeled momentarily. For each element that was blessed, this process was repeated. Once the elements on the table had been blessed, the 'synaxis' started praying the Lord's Prayer, the worshippers joined in with the 'synaxis' by praying altogether in monotone. Each member around the table then held up a cup as the priest prayed once more.

The remaining processes of the liturgical ritual of the Eucharist at Smuts Anglican were carried out in the usual manner, as described in the observations above. This includes the order in which worshippers go forward to receive, to the pianist announcing the songs of fellowship that will be sung whilst the worshippers (both adult and children) receive the Eucharist, to the worshippers praying in their preferred stances. A difference that was noticed at this observation, was that once every worshipper had received the Eucharist and after the children had partaken in the event, the deacon and 'synaxis' on duty took the elements to the pews of those that are not independently mobile so that they could also receive the Eucharist. This was not done in either of the previous worship services that were observed. While it was being done, another of the clergy on duty was emptying the cups and rinsing them with a bit of water at the table. The cups were then wiped with a cloth and placed next to the plates, all of which were then covered with a large, white cloth. After they covered the elements of the Eucharist with the cloth, the priest; deacon and 'synaxis' waited behind the altar while the choir finished the song they were singing. Once the singing had come to an end, the priest began a prayer which was concluded by a response by the worshippers. After the prayer, the priest asked for the notices to be read. At this point one of the worshippers went forward, to the lectern, to read the notices. There was one announcement that was particularly worth mentioning, the worshipper reading the notices announced that anyone in need of prayer, to please come to the front of the church where they would be met by a member of 'the prayer ministry' team at the end of the service.

It has been noticed that in previous observations the worship service becomes quite informal from the beginning of the reading of the notices. In this more casual regard, the priest mentioned to the worshippers that he would like to pray for two people who were celebrating their birthdays the next day. He also requested that the cakes, brought for one of the worshipper's birthday, be brought forward so that may be prayed for. Before praying for the cakes, the priest asked the deacon to join him in prayer. His prayer included the phrase "Bless this treat for the church . . . "

As the worship service came to a conclusion, the priest requested that the worshippers recite the prayer for Africa, after which was the announcement of the closing hymn. Similarly to the previous observations, the worshippers stood as the priest and the rest of the clergy left the church via the aisle. Once they were outside they joined hands, in a circle surrounding a lit candle, and shared a brief prayer. As the closing hymn ended, the worshippers began leading out the church, each one being greeted by a member of the clergy as they walked out the doors and onto the path where the priest and clergy were waiting.

2.2.1.4. Conclusion of the observed worship services at Smuts Anglican

The most prominent similarity is the use of the An Anglican Prayer Book as well as the number of prayers in each worship service. In the first worship service, there were twelve observed prayers. These prayers included prayers from the prayer book; a prepared prayer by the 'synaxis'; silent, individual prayers by the worshippers; the Lord's prayer; the Prayer for Africa as well as extemporaneous prayers made by the priest and worshippers whom he asked to join him. One of the prayers was a prayer for the church administrator that was led by the priest and four worshippers whom he requested to join him.

The second worship service that was observed, which described eleven occasions of prayer, similar to the examples given above. It was also noticed that the clergy prayed just outside the door of the church, once they had led out of the building as the worshippers sang the final hymn/song of fellowship. There was also an invitation, in the form of an announcement when the notices were being read, for those needing prayer to go to the front of the church at the end of the worship service where they would be met by a member of the 'prayer ministry'.

In the final worship service that was attended and described above, there were fourteen mentions of prayer. This, like with the second description, excluded a prayer that was observed of the clergy praying on the pathway outside the door of the church while waiting for the worshippers to lead out of the church. Included in the fourteen mentioned prayers were most of the examples given above as well as the priest praying for two worshippers who had birthdays the following day and for birthday cakes that were provided by one of the worshippers.

Across the three worship services there were thirty-seven prayers observed, this is an average of twelve prayers per worship service. Considering that the worship service is approximately one and a half hours in duration, there is then a prayer started every seven minutes on average. Many of these prayers are directly from the aforementioned prayer book, this will be discussed in the next chapter. Other normative discussions and interpretations such as: the Collect(s), the Lord's Prayer and the Prayer for Africa will also be discussed when considering the normative task of practical theological interpretation.

The strict following of the liturgy in the prayer book brought forward many similarities. It also brought light to some topics for discussion. The first of which is the strong sense of liturgical tradition at the church, the prayer book used was published in 1989 thus questions should be asked: (1) how inculturated is the liturgy seen as the twenty-plus year old prayer book and its liturgy are still being used? And (2) where does culture(s) of worshippers' fit in to the church and its liturgy? Furthermore, the constant use of the more dated choir and organ as apposed to more modern alternatives provides further insight into the strong sense of liturgical tradition. The use of the choir, organ and piano are certainly a tradition of the church and need not necessarily be adapted for the (pop)cultural wants of the worshippers however the question should be asked—in the interpretive task: how well does the culture(s) of worshippers connect to such a tradition? The main aim of this chapter is to describe the empirical data hence these questions are left unanswered as they will be addressed in later chapters that focus on interpretation.

2.2.2. What is Going on in the Worship Services at Titans Church

Titans Church, as mentioned earlier, serves as the charismatic church for this study. It is a not a mega church with a massive auditorium but rather a quaint, simple building which is similar in size to Smuts Anglican. The church does well to exude excitement from before the worship service begins, until it is finished. In comparison to Smuts Anglican, it is a more jovial place with a lot more 'noise'. The word 'noise' is used in the sense that the worshippers socialise outside the church, before the worship service, and continue in a similar vain as they enter the church and greet familiar faces until the worship service begins. 'Noise' is also used in the sense that the music, during worship, has a high level of production value and theatre to it. Lastly, the word 'noise' explains the worshippers that shout out in prayer as they worship. The sense of bricolage at Titans Church is also rather minimal, the musical instruments used are what is likely to be expected from a charismatic church. There is also a good use of technology, not only in the use of data projectors and sound equipment but also multimedia technology such as animated slide shows and a live countdown, which will be described in the individual worship service descriptions below.

At Titans Church, there is no book dictating an order of service like that of Smuts Anglican. However, the order of service—or agenda—at each of the worship service observations remained constant. Another similarity through all the worship services was the open displays of emotion from various parties such as: the pastor, the MC, members of the worship band and individual worshippers amongst the congregation. The 'noise' referred to above, also explains these emotional displays ranging from laughter and shouting out in joy, to tears and expressions of sorrow.

The worship services, in general, were rather compartmentalised. There was a time dedicated to worship, time dedicated to announcements and sharing of testimonies and time dedicated to the sermon. The only aspect that was not compartmentalised in full was prayer. Prayers seemed to happen as the relevant parties felt it necessary.

The time for worshipping contributed to a majority of the worship service. It was a lot more free, open and expressive than at the previously observed, Smuts Anglican. During the time(s) of worship, the worshippers did not simply sing along with the band—there were no communal, conformal liturgical ritual acts but rather personal ones. What was observed were more individual liturgical ritual acts that were performed as the worshipper was experiencing the worship for him/herself.

By describing what is going on at each of the observed worship services, more similarities will arise. Above is an introduction to the church, along with some similarities that aid in setting the scene. There are some questions that have arisen from this introduction that will be combined with questions arising from the similarities provided after the below descriptions. All of these questions will be answered through interpretation in the later chapters.

2.2.2.1. First Observation at Titans Church

The worship service began with a song of worship as the worshippers made their way, from chatting outside, to their seats inside the church. There was a worship band consisting of: a drummer, keyboardist, bass guitarist and another keyboardist who was also the lead vocalist. The band was placed around the stage, underneath and in between two screens, on which two data projectors shone the lyrics to the worship song. This worship service marked the beginning of a new preaching series.

After entering the church, the worshippers stood in front of their chairs and joined the band in song. At the end of the song, a master of ceremonies (MC) went up onto the stage and asked the worshippers to open their Bibles and read a verse from Hebrews 2. Following this reading, a large number of worshippers began to pray out loud. They prayed as individuals in a gracious, extemporaneous yet repetitive manner as the band continued with the song of worship with which the worship service had begun. During the song, there were worshippers who had their hands raised in different poses. Some had their arms extended above their heads, while others had their hands held up—palms facing to them—at chest level. It was noticed that the majority of the worshippers were swaying from side to side as they sung along.

The pastor, who was standing in the front row of seats, was praying out loud. His prayer could be heard from the back of the church. He prayed a prayer similar to the song that was being sung, as the worshippers and band sung. His prayer was extemporaneous and was personal, it wasn't a prayer with the worshippers. The singing stopped and the music continued as the worshippers began praying—individually. The band then transitioned into the next song, the music is loud—the drummer beat away with no restraint. There was nothing meek or mild about the way worshipping through song had been conducted so far. It could be said that the worship service had started with a 'bang', there was an attitude of excitement shared by the band and the worshippers.

The MC stepped forward to pray again, while the band played their instruments without any vocals. Once the prayer was completed, the MC asked one of the worshippers to come forward and "share", adding the worshippers could get stuff off their chests. The MC warned that any worshippers that would like to share should first tell the MC, who would act as judge and decide whether it could or could not be shared. Besides the person that was called forward by the MC, only one other worshipper came forward to share an image he/she had while worshipping prior to the MC's invitation. Throughout this process, the band played their instruments with reserve in respect for those with a microphone—such as the MC and the two worshippers who came forward to "share." The band proceeded to the next song of worship as soon as the second worshipper was done sharing. Some of the worshippers had, voluntarily, sat down. Many of the worshippers that were standing had raised their hands above their heads as they sang. Once more there was a break in the singing, as the instruments continued being played, the pastor took to the stage to pray. The end of the prayer brought the MC to the stage, who asked the worship band to take their seats. He proceeded by announcing the notices. As he did so, the notices were displayed by the projectors on the two screens above the stage. A joke was made by the MC as there were two notices regarding outreach. The MC also announced the beginning of a new preaching series.

The MC called the pastor to the stage, he prayed with him before handing over to him. The pastor then began his address by asking one of the worshippers to come to the stage and share a vision they had just had during the worship session. The new preaching series is titled "Money, mission, margin." A graphic displaying the name was projected onto the two screens. Before the pastor began his sermon, he asked for the collection to be taken. This was done by the passing around of old-fashioned, tin 'cookie jars'. The pastor asked for the collection to be taken before the sermon, his reason being that he did not want the worshippers to feel forced to donate more than usual as a result of what he was going to preach about.

When meeting with the pastor, he mentioned that it would be more worthwhile to attend the 08:30 service as it was the fuller of the two worship services on a Sunday. The church is relatively small and was most likely around sixty percent capacity for this service.

During the service, the pastor repeatedly mentioned the phrase "The peace of God." The same phrase was also mentioned by the MC on several occasions. The pastor concluded the sermon by asking the worshippers to join with him by standing up. Once all the worshippers were standing, he began to pray. After the prayer, the pastor concluded his sermon by saying "God bless you" to the congregation.

Almost instantly, without any reservation, the worshippers began turning from their chairs and headed towards the exit of the church. While the worshippers were leaving the church, some contemporary Christian music was played from a laptop, through the large speakers at the front of the church, at the sound desk. Whilst worshippers were exiting the church, there was a couple that were praying together near the front of the church. It was also noted that a family had asked the pastor to pray with them, for their child. The pastor, surrounded by the family, laid his hands on the child as he prayed for him/her.

A Sense of Belonging

2.2.2.2. Second Observation at Titans Church

The worshippers were called into the church so that the worship service could begin. Immediately after the arrival of the worshippers, the first song of worship began. All the worshippers were standing at their seats and worshipping—led by the worship band. As this song ended, the MC—who is not the same person as the last observation—went forward and asked the worshippers to be seated. The MC then asked those who had recently returned from an outreach project in the Free State (another province in the Republic of South Africa), to come forward and share their experiences with the worshippers. The first person to speak, mentioned praying for the youth; while the second mentioned "Being doers." The third person shared that it was a blessing and wanted to do more. The fourth person mentioned 1 John 3:16 and explained to the worshippers that it's not just talking about it but actually helping 'them'. The fifth and final person spoke to the worshippers in attendance about "bonding" and "fellowship."

It was noticed that the church was slightly less full than at the previous observation, closer to fifty percent of its capacity. Also noted was that the worship band consisted of: a drummer, a bass guitarist, an electric guitarist, a keyboardist and two vocalists. After the people, who had been asked to share, were done the MC asked the worshippers to stand again and then quoted from Jeremiah 1. The worship band were playing their instruments while the MC addressed the worshippers and spoke about 'sending'—about mission workers and going out to the nations. The conclusion of the explanation cued the beginning of the next song of worship, the worshippers soon joined in—in singing—with the worship band. While there was a break in the vocals and only instruments being played, there were a few worshippers that were muttering along in what seemed to be prayer. Snippets of the muttering can be heard clearly as some of the worshippers are saying: " . . . love you Jesus." The worship leader, also the lead vocalist, addressed the worshippers briefly about lifting God up and continuing to praise Him this morning. The band continued with the same song as before the instrumental break. The song began to crescendo. The volume and intensity of the music constantly increased and decreased as a result of the worship band and what followed in the order of service. The worship leader then broke into prayer as the rest of the band continued to play and sing softly.

One of the worshippers went forward to the stage, addressed the worshippers using a microphone and explained a vision he/she had while stuck in traffic in his/her car. Again, while he/she spoke the band continued to play, in the background, in a soft respectful manner. The worshipper's experience was followed by the MC addressing the worshippers on "speaking out" the love of Jesus - "amazing King." The MC adds that "His love (Jesus') is overwhelming." A call was then made, by the MC, for anyone to share. The MC mentioned that, " Jesus will put words on your lips." The pastor could be heard shouting out in prayer: "Jesus . . . Jesus . . . Yes Jesus!" Shortly after the pastor's extemporaneous prayer, a worshipper went forward to share about a meeting he/she had during the week prior to the worship service. He/she explained how a friend complimented him/her on his/her 'loving heart'. The worship leader then took to the microphone, addressing the worshippers on "the fear to fail"—suggesting to the worshippers: "don't let things hold you back." Yet another worshipper came forward to share something with the worshippers, more specifically with the drummer: "The Holy Spirit says you'll be an amazing drummer."

To conclude this time of sharing, the MC asked the worshippers to bow their heads in prayer—and to raise their hands to "invite Jesus in." The MC began the prayer with, "You have spoken . . . " The MC shouted out while praying, swopping between addressing the worshippers and praying. The MC addressed the worshippers as if he/she was praying. This prayer bore plenty emotion. After the prayer, the MC asked the worshippers to be seated, the worship band took this as their queue to leave the stage, and their instruments, and be seated amongst the worshippers. Once everyone was seated, the MC proceeded with the notices. The MC announced that there would be two different offerings for this worship service: one was the normal offering (or collection) and the other was for the church's 'building fund'. After announcing all the notices, the MC took his seat. The pastor and one of the worshippers went up on stage. The worshipper announced that he/she would like to do a 'prophetic enactment' on the pastor "as the leader of the church." The worshipper tied a few thin chains around the pastor—chaining his arms and hands. He/she explained the analogy involving the chains and then proceeded to break the chains off of the pastor—freeing him, in a sense. The worshipper then 'prophesied' that the pastor and his family were released—their chains had been broken, "They can go out."

The pastor then proceeded with the sermon. At the end of the sermon, the pastor asked the worshippers to stand. The MC, who had arrived on stage again, asked for the worshippers to hold out their hands. They did so in the direction of the pastor and his family, as if they were laying hands on them. After the prayer, the MC mentioned that there will be tea and coffee after the worship service—in the courtyard adjacent to the church. The worshippers began to exit the church swiftly as some worship music was played through the church's sound system, from a CD or the computer at the sound desk. The majority of worshippers had left the church, there was a worshipper being prayed for, at the front of the church. The pastor and his wife had their hands laid on the worshipper as they prayed with him/her. The worship service, as in the previous observation, seemed to end abruptly. This is most likely due to the 10:30 service which follows from the 08:30 worship service.

2.2.2.3. Third Observation at Titans Church

Upon entering the church, the word 'welcome' was displayed on both of the projector screens above the stage. Underneath the word was a live countdown to the start of the worship service. While some of the worshippers had entered the church, and others were socializing outside, there was music playing through the sound system. The layout in the church was different, there were four trestle tables set up: two at the back of the church, along the back wall and then one in each front corner, just in front of the stage. Each of the tables had the elements for communion on them.

As the countdown ended, the worship band began with the first song of worship. The worship band consisted of: two vocalists, a keyboardist, an electric guitarist, a bass guitarist and a drummer. In comparison to the two prior worship services, the church was slightly emptier at about forty percent. While the band continued in leading the worshippers in worship, there were two door stewards that were still waiting at the door to greet those who arrived late. The worshippers, who entered the church in time to witness the end of the countdown, were worshipping after finding their way to their seats but not sitting down. As the countdown ended, the worship band began with the first song of worship. As the introductory song ended, the MC went up to the stage and immediately opened the worship service with a prayer. The MC only greeted the worshippers once he/she had said amen. After welcoming the worshippers to the service, the MC greeted all the visitors to the church.

The MC then announced to the worshippers that one of the members of the church had a nine month old baby that passed away. The MC added: " . . . we prayed and we trusted . . . and it wasn't meant to be." He/

she continued his/her address by praying for the pastor and his family that were travelling through the United States of America. After the prayer, the MC called one of the worshippers to the stage to explain that they will be doing communion during the worship service. The worshipper explained why 'we' do communion. This explanation included the history of the Greek word for 'communion' and that it also means "because of" or "instead of." The worshipper then prayed, as this happened the pianist and guitarist started playing one of the worship songs gently—as background music. As the prayer concluded, the music built in volume and the drummer joined in. Communion (the Eucharist), during this worship service, was available for every worshipper to partake in—there are no prerequisites. Each of the worshippers walked to the nearest table, broke a piece of bread for themselves and took a small glass of, what appeared to be, grape juice. No instructions were given on how this process works. Some worshippers gathered with their families and/or friends and bowed their heads in prayer. Other worshippers took the elements and returned to their seats. After a large number of the worshippers had taken their elements, a few volunteers walk around with buckets for the worshippers to put their empty glasses in.

Once all the worshippers, who chose to, had partaken in the communion, the MC went up on stage and announced: "Let us worship! Let us worship . . . Thank you Jesus." The majority of the worshippers were already standing, some with their hands raised above their heads. While the worship band repeated the bridge of the song they were singing, there were two or three worshippers that were standing with their heads bowed and their hands together in what looked like a prayer. They prayed alone and then proceeded to join in with the worship.

The worship in this service appeared to be slightly different to the two previous observations. The worship set seemed to be more of a medley and not as structured as was the case in the previous observations. There was a pause in the worship as the MC went on stage and asked all the men to stand. He/she proceeded to explain what God was telling him. The front doors, nearest the stage, were opened as many of the children from the 'kids' ministry' walked in. The children lined up across the front of the stage, each child had a sheet of paper in their hands, each with a piece of text on which the child in possession had to read. They read about the "unsung heroes" in the Bible. A slideshow was then played displaying a series of super heroes followed by a slideshow of all the dads, concluding with a 'happy father's day' message at the end of the presentations. There was a worshipper leading this presentation, who prayed briefly for all the fathers to be the men God wants them to be. After the prayer, the children went through all the rows of chairs and handed out a chocolate to each of the men in the church. The MC took over from the worshipper and the presentation, to continue, with the worship service and asked for all the tithes and offerings to be collected. The preacher for this worship service, who preached in the pastor's absence, prepared him/herself while the tithes and offerings were taken. The preacher began his/her sermon by announcing its title: "The father's heart." The title was displayed on the two projector screens above the stage. The topic and title of this sermon was appropriate due to it being Father's Day. The preacher explained six 'father types' in his/her sermon. The preacher also read from Luke 15:11–24, the parable of the prodigal son. The reason for using this passage of scripture was to explain that the parable has as great a lesson for the 'father' as it does for the 'son' because the 'father' was expecting the 'son's' return.

The sermon ended with a video clip, the preacher asked the worshippers to pay attention. The pastor mentioned that there would be a time for ministry at the end of the video clip. The clip was displayed on the two projector screens that have been mentioned above. To conclude the sermon, the preacher made an 'altar call'. As the 'altar call' was made, the keyboardist found his/her way to the keyboard and started playing gently and quietly. Four worshippers went forward to the stage, the MC aided the preacher in 'ministering' to the worshippers. The preacher was observed praying for one of the worshippers. He/she began praying for the worshipper by putting his/her left hand on the worshipper's shoulder, then putting his/her right hand on the worshipper's chest near the heart and finally moving the right hand on the worshipper's forehead before ending the prayer with 'amen'.

As the "time for ministry" came to an end with the ending of prayers, the MC declared: "Let us stand in worship." At this point, only the keyboardist was playing and singing. The drummer later joined the keyboardist, leaving his/her seat among the worshippers, by going on stage. Most of the worshippers were standing, there was a worshipper at the back of the church with eyes closed; head titled up toward the roof; arms folded and talking in prayer. At the end of this last period of worship, the MC prayed a thankful prayer. Before concluding his/her duties as MC, he/she announced that tea and coffee would be served outside and then closed the worship service with: "Thank you for joining us, bye!"

2.2.2.4. Conclusion of the observed worship services at Titans Church

The most prominent observation across all three worship services was that there was no strict liturgical order that was followed, each worship service varied. For example, only in one worship service was there communion. The liturgy at Titans Church is far less rigid than at, the previously observed, Smuts Anglican. Another more notable similarity was that the worship services are music orientated. What is meant by this is that for the majority of the worship service(s), there was music being played in one form or another. In some instances music was played due to the worship requirements, yet for the majority of addresses by the various masters of ceremony there was music being played in the background. A similar case appeared when the MC, or anyone else who made use of a microphone, was praying. It could be summarized that there were two main instances when music was not being played, the first would be during the sermon and secondly when the notices were being announced.

In the first worship service observation, there were seven occasions where the worshippers were subjected to prayer. The reason for using the word 'subjected' is due to the prayers that were not directly part of the liturgy. For example, on occasions throughout all three worship service observations, the pastor would exclaim in prayer—the same can be said of a few worshippers as well as some of the worship band members. During the second worship service observation, the worshippers were subjected to prayer considerably less than at the first worship service observation. This being on only four occasions.

Perhaps coincidentally, the third worship service observation also described seven occasions where the worshippers were subjected to prayer—the same as the first worship service observation. In summation, the majority of prayers are conducted by the MC on duty. On average there are six prayers per worship service. The worship service(s) is about ninety minutes from start to finish, meaning there is a prayer started, on average, once every fifteen minutes. In comparison to the Anglican Church, whose worship services were observed, there is one prayer at Titans Church for every two prayers at Smuts Anglican. It should also be noted that none of the prayers at Titans Church are from a book, all the prayers are rather extemporaneous in nature. Also some of the prayers considered for the averages given above are not prayers that are made from the stage but simply worshippers, the pastor or worship leader that prayed in their own space and time—not necessarily for the worshippers to participate in but certainly audible enough for all to be subjected to. The prayers, made from the stage and intended for everyone in the church, may have been written and rehearsed before hand but none of them are from any sort of worship manual. This is not to say that either method is preferred or superior to the other, it is simply an observation.

A less important similarity, although still interesting to mention, is that the sermon—in all three worship services—was the last item on the agenda. The entire worship service built up to the sermon. In all three descriptions, the worship service was ended shortly and suddenly following the end of the sermon. As the opportunity arises to compare one church's liturgy to another, so more questions are left to be answered by the chapters that follow. In the interim, it is necessary to proceed to the worship service observations of the mainline congregation in the form of Hennops Methodist.

2.2.3. What is Going on in the Worship Services at Hennops Methodist

Hennops Methodist served as the mainline congregation. Out of the three churches, this church displayed the highest amount of bricolage. In one worship service there was a traditional African church choir, in another there was a worship band and in the third observation there was a worship band that included an organ. With regard to prescribed liturgy, this church follows, roughly, a predetermined and generic order of service. This point, however, is something that will be discussed in detail when doing the normative task in a later chapter. From a cultural perspective, Hennops Methodist displayed an engagement with more than one culture not only by using a traditional African church choir but by, with the assistance of the choir, singing worship songs in an African vernacular or two. Coincidentally, one of the worship service observations was done on the Sunday before the South African municipal elections. This was not the only instance where the focus was on the South African context, however, it is a good example of the importance of said context to the church.

Hennops Methodist, like Titans Church, makes use of information technology by using data projectors and electronic sound equipment. They also make use of multimedia technology by displaying greetings before the service starts, as well as presenting the notices in the form of a news bulletin style presentation, that will be described below. All worship song lyrics, Bible readings and reciprocal prayers are displayed on the projector screens. This church has the largest building of the three churches, which directly influences the number of worshippers that are at the worship services. The number of worshippers at Hennops Methodist is much larger than that of the other two churches. For this reason there are three worship services per Sunday. It was decided that the 09h45 worship service would be observed as it was the worship service that was attended by all the interviewees from Hennops Methodist. From a methodological perspective, it was imperative to attend the worship service that was described and discussed by the interviews in order to develop a better understanding of what goes on in the worship service at this church.

A major similarity across all three worship service observations was a token called 'the Family Cross'. This item is given to a person or family that are experiencing one or other type of hardship. It is presented on a weekly basis and announced during the worship service. The aim behind handing this to said person or family is for them to know that God, assumedly, as well as the worshippers present in the service are with them in thought and prayer as they experience their hardship. Discretion is used but the circumstances of the person or family were usually explained before it was requested of the worshippers to consider this person and/or family and pray for them throughout the week. Another similarity, or technique, that was found through all three worship services was the minister's way of addressing the worshippers, constantly referring to them as 'friends'. This along with the importance of the "Family Cross" are examples of the sense of fellowship in the church that was observed during participation in the worship services. The same minister led and preached at all three of the worship services.

2.2.3.1. *First Observation at Hennops Methodist*

The worship service began at 09:45 with a traditional African choir on the stage. They were singing songs of praise while the worshippers entered the church. The pianist then asked the worshippers to stand and join in song with the choir. At the end of this song, the minister went on stage and asked the worshippers to be seated and as they did so he/she asked the worshippers to greet those around them. This was followed by a short introduction and welcome to the worship service. The minister then announced that the news clip would be shown. The clip was a produced video that was displayed on the two projector screens from data projectors. Once the production ended, the minister added to the announcements in the news clip with a few of his/her own. The minister followed the announcements with a Bible reading from Jeremiah, followed by a prayer. The aforementioned choir were standing behind the minister, on the stage, while he/she made his/her introduction; announcements; reading and prayer. Once the prayer was completed, the minister asked the worshippers to stand "as we worship together."

The African choir, with accompaniment from the pianist, led the worshippers in worship. The choir was a traditional-type African choir, the way they sung was different to the choir at Smuts Anglican. There were plenty of verbose harmonies that were not appealing to the ear of the worshippers and happened randomly, making it difficult for the worshippers to follow. At the end of the second worship song, one of the choir members began to pray, making references to 'Jehovah'. As an example of this utterances 're-ceive our prayers, Jehovah' were heard. This prayer was followed by a third worship song, in an African language. The first two worship songs were in English and were more popular with the worshippers.

A prayer was said after the third song, by the minister, as the pianist played soft background music. At the end of the prayer, the minister asked the worshippers to be seated. The minister went on to explain that the upcoming week was an important one in South Africa, by speaking around the topic of the municipal elections without mentioning the term. It was announced that a period of open prayer would happen for the upcoming elections. The minister began this period of prayer, quickly followed by a series of worshippers. It was noted that there were no long pauses, barely any pauses at all, between the end of one worshipper's prayer and the beginning of the next worshipper's prayer. The minister also closed the prayer, after waiting for anyone else to pray with no avail. Following this period of prayer, the minister suggested that the offering would be taken "as an act of worship." This was followed by an instruction to remain seated until the worshippers' contributions had been given. While the offering was taken the choir sang, starting with an English song of worship. The singing came across as quite unappealing, however it was certainly a more African traditional approach as those that speak African languages were reveling in the experience and seemed to know when to harmonize like the choir were. The worshippers stood and joined in with the worship after giving their contributions or passing the bag to the next worshipper.

The minister asked the worshippers to be seated, once the taking of the collection was completed. His/her request was also the choir and pianist's queue to leave the stage. The minister began his/her address by announcing that before the "Family Cross" is handed to the next recipient, he/she would like to read a 'thank you' letter from a previous recipient. In the letter, read by the minister, the recipient thanks the church (and worshippers) for all their prayers and the "power of prayer." The minister then called the new recipient to the stage and asked that whoever would like to pray with the recipient to go forward and lay hands.

After completing this aspect of the worship service, the minister proceeded to the sermon and began with a Bible verse. The minister mentioned that this Bible verse, Psalm 32:3–5 was very personal to him/her. The sermon was the third of a preaching series titled "Twelve Step Program." Introducing the sermon, the minister states that "All of us are addicted to sin." A segment of a video clip was shown, it was a pastor/priest's explanation of his struggle with sin. Following the segment, the minister explained that today's sermon is about the fifth step in this twelve step program. He/she continued by revising the first four steps. Towards the end of the sermon, another segment—later in the story told by the pastor/priest—was shown. While this second portion of the video was shown, the choir and pianist returned to the stage.

Once the video clip ended, the minister said "Let us pray." As the minister ended his/her address, the following announcement was made: "If you feel the need to pray, you may go to the rail after the service where there will be people to pray with you." The closing hymn was a sung version of the Prayer for Africa. The worshippers were requested to stand and join the choir, before the song was started. After the hymn, the minister called for the benediction and explained that after it the national anthem of South Africa would be sung. The minister mentioned that 'Nkosi Sikelela' was originally written as a prayer by a Methodist pastor.

Before the worshippers exited the church, upon completion of the worship service, it was noted that the church was at about ninety percent of its capacity. There were few empty seats.

2.2.3.2. Second Observation at Hennops Methodist

The introductory worship song was "Lord reign in me", most likely as a result of the rainfall the night before and used because of the homophone. At the end of the song, the minister greeted the worshippers before quickly moving on to a prayer. The prayer was followed by the minister's suggestion that the worshippers greet those around them. Once sufficient time had been given for the worshippers to greet one another, the minister announced "The Hennops Methodist News." These notices were presented in the same multimedia, news bulletin style presentation as the previously observed worship service. While the presentation was broadcasted on the projector screens, it was noted that the church was not nearly as full as at the previous observation at approximately sixty percent.

Proceeding the news, the worship leader asked the worshippers to stand. The worship band consisted of a drummer; an acoustic guitarist; a bass guitarist and three vocalists. The first worship song was quietly followed by the worshippers. The second song was better received by the worshippers, their voices could actually be heard instead of just the band, especially during the chorus. The response was not only audibly evident but the increased interest could also be seen by watching worshippers swaying from side to side, while others raised their hands above their heads. The end of the second song led to the worship leader praying, proceeded by a third song. At this point, some of the worshippers took it upon themselves to sit down—of which some worshippers sat in order to pray.

At the end of the next song, the worship leader announced that "we will continue in worship by taking the tithes and offerings." The worshippers were asked to be seated, they begin to stand and join in song with the worship band as they placed their contributions in the bags being passed around. Once all contributions had been collected, the society steward on duty prayed for the collection. The conclusion of the prayer and the arrival of the minister on stage subliminally instructed the worshippers to take their seats as well as the worship band leaving the stage for their seats too. The minister was standing behind a lectern of sorts, a music stand, while the wooden lectern was against a wall on the side of the stage. Near it was a wooden table, with a crossed placed in the centre with a burning candle in front of it.

This worship service marked the beginning of a new preaching series entitled "Caution, Highly Addictive" which was displayed on the two projector screens at the front of the church. The sermon was about being cautious of money and its addictiveness. Throughout the sermon, the minister addressed the worshippers as 'friends'. It was noted above that the number of worshippers was considerably less than in the previous observed worship service. The minister explains to the worshippers that were present that the church is less full today due to many worshippers attending a thanksgiving service at another church. At the end of the sermon, the minister asked: "Let us pray together." While the minister led the worshippers in prayer, the worship band returned to their positions on stage. At the end of the prayer, the minister asked the worshippers to stand "as we worship God together."

All of this service's worship songs were in English. After the latest worship song, the worship leader announced: "We are going to pray right now." The worship service was concluded by the worshippers joining hands and saying the benediction together.

2.2.3.3. Third Observation at Hennops Methodist

Upon entering the church, before the worship service began, there was a message displayed on the two projector screens at the front of the church saying: "We're glad you're here" and "Welcome to church." The worship band was slightly different to the previous participatory observation, consisting of: an organist, an acoustic guitarist, an electric bass guitarist and two male vocalists—both played the respective guitars. Just before the worship service began, the minister; worship band and two other men joined hands and prayed on the stage.

The minister opened the worship service by greeting the worshippers with "Good morning friends" and welcomed them to the worship service. As in the previous participatory observations, the news bulletin was then announced and played in the same multimedia format on the two projector screens. While this production was on, it was noted that the church was at about seventy-five percent of its capacity with worshippers sporadically entering the church to join the worship service. After the news bulletin, the minister made another announcement. While the announcement was being made, the words "Let us pray" were displayed on the two projector screens. Before praying, as suggested by the display on the projector screens, the minister presented the "Family Cross" and asked the worshippers to keep the recipient family in their prayers.

Once the suggested prayer was completed, the minister asked the worshippers to stand as they worshipped by joining in song. The worshippers stood and quietly sang along with the worship band, for the first song. The second song was met by a considerably louder voice from the worshippers. The minister suggested: "Let us worship in prayer" and prayed between the second and third worship song. The third song was also met by a substantial voice from the worshippers. The volume of the song came and went which displayed the familiarity of certain points of the song such as the chorus. As the song progressed the worship band built in crescendo, however the worshippers' voice seemed to fade in an almost despondent manner. The volume of their voice did return when the chorus was sung again. Once again, at the end of the third worship song, the minister stepped forward to pray. The prayer was followed by a fourth worship song, many of the worshippers followed along with their arms folded across their chests. As with the end of the second and third worship songs, the fourth worship song was followed by another prayer from the minister. It was a prayer for forgiveness. Upon saying "amen", the minister asked the worshippers to be seated before explaining that the worship service involved the baptism of five children.

The minister moved directly on to the ritual processes of the baptisms, by reading from the Methodist Service Book. The relevant text was displayed on the two projector screens for the worshippers' convenience. The convenience was that the worshippers could follow along and were aware of when they needed to respond. After the five baptisms, the worshippers read a blessing that was displayed for all to read. The blessing was followed by a "congregational response", which was also displayed on the screens.

Once all the families involved in the baptism had returned to their seats, the minister announced that the worship service would continue with one of the worshippers going forward to share their testimony. After the sharing of the testimony, the minister announced the taken of the offering. Similarly to the previous two participatory observations, the worshippers took to their feet, joining the worship band in song, after they had added their contributions to the bags and passed them along. Once all the bags had been collected and taken to the altar, the society steward on duty prayed for the offerings. As the society steward prayed, the organ was played softly in the background. The minister then requested that the worshippers be seated. A quick announcement was made before the minister proceeded with the sermon, beginning with a reading from Matthew 5:10.

This passage was displayed on the projector screens for the worshippers' convenience. The minister's sermon was associated with the earlier baptisms. In ending the sermon, the minister prayed while making a variety of hand gestures.

Following the prayer, the minister asked the worshippers to stand for the closing "hymn." After the closing "hymn", the minister asked the worshippers to join hands for the benediction. Before this request was made, the minister made an announcement for those needing prayer to go to the rails after the service. The benediction marked the end of the worship service. Upon completion of the benediction, the worshippers immediately turned from their seats and headed for the exits at the rear of the church. The worship band continued to perform as the worshippers exited the church. There were five groups of worshippers that went to the rails and were met by volunteers who prayed with them. Once the worship band had completed the song they were performing, they put down their instruments and began packing up. While the worship band were busy packing away their equipment, there were still worshippers being prayed for at the rails.

2.2.3.4. Conclusion of the observed worship services at Hennops Methodist

The most prominent similarity is the liturgical bricolage. Each worship service observation saw a different type of worship band. Not only were different instruments used, instruments that are not typically used together in a band were used. This alludes to an emphasis on cultural context. Making use of a more traditional African choir in the worship service leading up to the municipal elections is an example of this. Combining the organ with guitars and drums in the last worship service observed was evidence of mixing the old with the new in what is referred to as 'the family service'. This raises a question pertaining to the relationship between culture and tradition and where they meet at this church. Another strong similarity is that there was no communion in any of the three observed worship services. However there was a mass baptism, the word 'mass' is used to describe the fact that five young children and babies were baptized one after the other in the worship service. The object of this research project is prayer, therefore it should be discussed. In the first worship service observation, eight prayers were noted. The majority of these prayers were conducted by the minister at various stages in the worship service. Other contributors were the society steward who prayed after the offering was taken and one of the choir members who prayed between songs. One of the eight prayers in this worship service was the Prayer for Africa, which was sung by the worshippers but is a prayer nonetheless. Uniquely to the observations at Hennops Methodist, was that one of the prayers in this worship service was an open invitation prayer. The minister began and ended the prayer with a series of worshippers praying out loud from their seats between the minister opening and closing the prayer.

The second worship service that was observed noted five prayers. Once more these prayers were mainly conducted by the minister, with exception from the society steward and the worship leader. The third and final worship service observation noted nine prayers. Again contributions were made by the society steward and worship leader, with the majority being conducted by the minister. Overall twenty-two prayers were observed and noted across the three participatory observations. The worship services were all approximately 75 minutes in duration. Averaging just over seven prayers per worship service, there was a prayer started approximately every ten minutes.

From the perspective of fellowship and community there were two striking concepts from the worship service. The first is that, when addressing the worshippers, the minister used the word 'friends'. The second concept is that of the "Family Cross" which is given by the church to a predetermined worshipper or family that was determined by the church as being in a time of needing prayer. As noticed through the three descriptive summaries above, the minister led the service from start to finish. Typically the minister's prayers were extemporaneous in nature, so were the prayer's made by various worship team members and the society steward(s) on duty. Besides these prayers being extemporaneous, they were also relatively contextual. Each prayer was not only relevant in context to what was happening in the church during that specific week but also what was going on in the city, province and country around the time(s) of the worship services that were observed. For example: in the first worship service the minister (as well as some worshippers) were noted as praying for the country and its leadership, leading up to the municipal elections. There were also prayers for relief from the drought in the country and consequently rainfall. Many of these prayers came between songs during worship.

One last similarity is the announcements made by the minister for a prayer ministry after the worship service. The minister announced that those in need of prayer should go to the front of the church at the end of the service. It was observed that such worshippers were met by volunteers who prayed with/for them. The context of prayers was mentioned above which led to a question, according to Chupungco's candle analogy where to tradition—of the church—and culture (context) of the people meet? As with other questions posed in previously, this question will be addressed in the following chapters.

The aim of presenting these comprehensive descriptions was to describe certain episodes, situations and contexts which exhibited the lex orandi and/or lex credendi. The following section of this chapter deals with describing 'what is going on' from the perspective of the worshippers who volunteered to be interviewed. In this regard another term can be used for 'perspective', namely appropriation which refers to the manner in which society appropriates the worship service through a process of giving meaning to what is being experienced (bottom-up). By including the interviewees this chapter moves from designation, the same liturgy being discussed by a third party (or 'top-down'), to appropriation. The intention of describing various pieces of information and themes, in the next section, is to provide insight into the worshippers' perspectives as well as raise questions that should be examined and discussed in the proceeding chapters. The theory behind interviewing volunteering worshippers is that prayer is not something that only happens while attending a worship service on a Sunday at church. Prayer is a part of one's private life as well, an educated assumption that was backed up by the interviewees' accounts as prayer is an important aspect of the relationship between worshipper and God. This theory is related to the two questions posed in the introduction: "what beliefs (*lex credendi*) are exhibited by the worship manuals (*lex orandi*)?" and "what beliefs are exhibited (*lex credendi*) by peoples' prayers (*lex orandi* and *lex (con)vivendi*)?"

2.3. A PRAYING PEOPLE

One of the research aims was to determine whether people perceive that they can connect with God and fellow worshippers through prayer. For this to be determined worship services could not simply be observed, worshippers had to discuss whether they experienced connections or not. The aim of this section is to describe the themes, otherwise known as episodes, situations and contexts, that arose from the interviews. Below are a collection of themes that were discovered as a result of the interviews. These themes, as well as the similarities from the above worship service observations, will be used within their respective episodes, situations and contexts for the interpretive processes of this research project. Most of the themes, described below, are as a direct result of the semi-structured interview questions.

2.3.1. Quiet Times and Other Daily Rituals

The first question of each interview asked if the interviewee(s) pray and how often. In most cases the answer was a resounding 'yes' to whether or not the interviewee(s) engaged in prayer. The second part of the answer was usually a description of how often and what periods of the day each interviewee prayed. When collecting and sifting through the transcribed data, a popular term or theme was a daily ritual commonly referred to as "quiet time." The term is used to describe an individual's regular sessions of spiritual activity. 'Quiet time' is widely used in the Christian context and while there isn't an exact definition, if one Christian was to mention the term to another, the concept would be understood clearly.

Many of the interviewees detail what happens during their 'quiet times', thus painting a picture of what 'quiet time' is. There is a personal and private element to 'quiet time', therefore for each interviewee/worshipper it means something unique. For the majority of interviewees, who mention having or doing 'quiet time', it appeared to be a daily ritual. The data collected for this study suggests that the majority of interviewees, that make reference to 'quiet time', pray during their 'quiet time'. This is as a result of the number of references to 'quiet time' when explaining how often one prays. As an example of the above, John explained the following: "I try and pray in the mornings, quiet time when everybody has left the house . . . " For this interviewee, prayer and 'quiet time' are synonymous. It was also important for the interviewee to mention that his/her 'quiet time' is done when everybody has left the house. This could be for many reasons, among which that the interviewee is unable to be distracted when performing this more personal ritual encounter. His/her reasons for doing so when everyone else had left the house were not explained. Thomas also mentioned: "I have my quiet time in the morning . . . end off with a prayer." While neither interviewee provided an in-depth explanation into what exactly their 'quiet time' consists of, based on their explanations of prayer and other descriptions throughout the interviews, the two would agree that certain aspects of their respective 'quiet times' are similar but are unique and personal to each of them thus there should be many differences between the two accounts.

Both of the above mentioned interviewees also spoke about having 'quiet time' in the morning and praying in the evening, at the end of the day, in bed. Matthew doesn't make use of the term 'quiet time' but explained the following: " . . . certainly more formally in the morning and in the evening—you know, kind of getting up and going to bed time." Each of these three interviewees make use of prayer to start and end their day. On the contrary, and further adding to what 'quiet time' could be, Jude described that his/her 'quiet time' involved daily readings with no mention of prayer. Jude's description of 'quiet time' consisted more of reading devotional literature or Bible passages taken from the worship services. The idea behind each of the interviewees' rituals is similar, yet the execution is unique to each of them.

In each of the accounts above there is an undertone of routine. Andrew uses the word 'routine' in his/her explanation of how often he/she prays, to quote: " . . . it's also a daily routine for me, I try to pray as early as possible 'cause I'm at the office at six o'clock in the morning so there's nothing there. So it helps me to be quiet . . . " This interviewee also describes a ritual that differs from those given above, which is illustrated in the quotation below taken from the transcription: "I do walk as well now . . . normally I go cycle so I have time to be loud in the veld, there's no noise . . . And I talk more to God than I pray."

First of all, Andrew mentions his/her daily routine as time to be quiet and then mentions being loud when referring to the latter ritual. Again this is personal, private and not discussed in detail. These two quotations, in answering the same question, leave a question: Why does Andrew feel the need to be quiet with his/her daily routine and then loud in the veld? It was also important for the interviewee to mention that he/she talks to God more than he/she prays whilst in the veld, which is an example of ritual space. The noise, or opportunity to be loud, in the veld could be as a result of the interviewee only being able to disturb the peace of him/herself as there is no one else around. Whereas his/her quiet time, whether at the office or at home, may disturb the peace of those around the interviewee should he/she choose to be loud. The method behind these decisions could be due to consideration of others as well as the interviewee's pride and privacy.

Consideration for others and not wanting to disrupt anyone else is one aspect. The other aspect, one's pride or privacy, could be the interviewee's desire to not perform in front of anyone else. The difference between these two, specific, rituals is something that will be interpreted through the lenses of Ritual Studies in the next chapter.

Phillip makes mention of the following with regard to prayer routines: "I pray every morning without fail; I pray every evening without fail . . ." Starting and ending the day with prayer has been mentioned above and is a common theme from the interviews, thus illustrating that there are specific, perhaps cyclical, times for these rituals. While Phillip doesn't make a specific mention to 'quiet time', he/she does explain that his/her prayer process begins with finding a "quiet spot" or "quiet place" and then praying by talking to God. In two instances the interviewee mentions: (1) " . . . and when I pray it's like a communication that I have like I'm talking to you now . . . " and (2) "I talk to God like I'm talking to you now." These phrases are similar to Andrew's explanation of what occurs when he/she is in the veld, above.

From the above, there are two different aspects with regard to a relationship between the person praying (interviewee) and God. The first aspect is the importance laid on the relationship through the keenness to pray as one's day begins and then praying again at the end of the day. The second aspect is the emphasis, by some of the interviewees, on 'talking' to God when praying. This second aspect is something that comes more to the fore when investigating prayer, due to the evidence of a more human-type relationship. Specifically speaking, Interviewee mentions: "I talk to God like I'm talking to you now." The 'you' being the interviewer, a mere mortal. Throughout the interview with Jude a large amount of awe, respect and superiority can be seen when Jude speaks of God. Therefore there is no denying, from the side of Jude, that God for him/her is in fact a deity. The interviewee speaks of God's sovereignty on many occasions, however by talking to God as if talking to a human describes a relationship between two humans. This leaves much room for interpretation as well as debate but, at surface level, it also describes a clear connection or the perception thereof.

A further similarity between Andrew and Jude is the contents of their morning prayers. Both of the interviewees find it of paramount necessity to thank God for being alive, for being able to live another day. While Andrew and Jude give thanks, in prayer, for the day ahead, John takes to prayer in the evening to unpack the day that has unfolded: " . . . that's possibly why I have very meaningful prayer in the evening because it's what's, kind of, come through the day . . . " John spoke about questioning the day's events or issues. Perhaps he/she decompresses his/her thoughts or feelings experienced throughout the day through praying in the evening "while I'm lying in bed."

Before proceeding to the next theme, there was a common thread throughout the majority of the interviews that relates to daily prayer rituals. This is the common explanation(s) of praying throughout the day. As one would contact a loved one or friend as throughout the day so, many of the interviewees, contact God through prayers. Below are a number of quotes from the interviewees:

- Matthew: " . . . you must pray everyday, or all day everyday . . . "
- Peter: "I engage in prayer all day."
- Peter: "I mean, He's my everything so I have to be able to talk to Him all the time. So, for me prayer is very important and it's just an ongoing thing, all day—throughout my day."
- Andrew: "And during the day, I will get messages from people that said . . . I found I can sit behind my desk, my computer in front of me and I can pray. I can pray . . . while I'm driving . . . But I've found . . . even though the radio is on or there's someone else in the car, I can praise God . . . "
- Simon: "Most probably half a dozen times a day."
- Thomas: " . . . and then the rest of the time . . . just these little prayers to God when I need something, or I see something that's pretty . . . "
- Phillip: "Yes I do engage in prayer and at every opportunity that I can 'cause I don't only pray for things when I ask of God."
- Phillip: "So I pray to God, I don't want to say three times; four times; five times but I pray to God regularly. I pray every morning without fail; I pray every evening without fail and during the day I also pray—perhaps not on my knees but I pray. I have relationship and constant contact with God."

Some key phrases from the above quotations that describe the magnitude of praying throughout the day are: "I have relationship and constant contact with God", " . . . all day everyday . . . ", " . . . prayer is very important and it's just an ongoing thing, all day—throughout my day.", "Every opportunity." When looking at how one perceives their relationship with God, the importance of praying throughout the day or being in "constant contact with God" is a relative point of departure when looking at the interviewees' perceptions of God's role in their lives and ultimately their relationship with God. The term 'relationship' is used as it was something mentioned by many of the interviewees. In order to gain insight into these perceptions, the contents of the prayers—as told by the interviewees—need to be examined. This is something that will be done in a later theme which will deal more with the contents of prayers and not the ritual dimension of praying.

What can be derived up to this point is that there are two main types of prayer rituals that have been discovered. The first being 'structured' especially in reference to a dedicated time, commonly referred to as 'quiet time'. The second type of ritual, or rituals, is 'unstructured' in the sense that it relies on spontaneity depending on events throughout the day. A case could be made that the 'structured' rituals are in fact a ritual and that the 'unstructured' are not, however a ritual is still performed albeit in a more spontaneous nature. This topic will be discussed and interpreted through the lenses of Ritual Studies in the next chapter. An aspect strongly related to these 'unstructured' rituals is the theme of extemporaneous prayers. These are prayers that are not prescribed nor from any prayer manual. The next theme to be discussed is extemporaneous prayers.

2.3.2. Extemporaneous Prayers

There is a relationship between the 'unstructured' rituals explained above and extemporaneous prayers. This ritual type is synonymous with extemporaneous prayers, in this case the former exists because of the latter. Without extemporaneous prayers, there would be no 'unstructured' rituals to discuss here. It should be noted that a number of interviewees make use of, what will be described as, prayer guides. These prayer guides aid the interviewees in following a specific pattern and are not relevant when discussing the contents of extemporaneous prayers. Prayer guides form a separate theme and will be discussed as such at a later stage in this chapter. The contents of extemporaneous prayers are personal and relative to the individual. The contents of such prayers are therefore deemed necessary to pray about by each interviewee. One interviewee may pray about certain things that another interviewee could think are unnecessary to pray about. Such is the nature of extemporaneous prayers.

While discussing the nature of these prayers, a good example of the personal relevance thereof is the way in which John prays in the evening while reflecting on the day that has past. Although this evening prayer, spoken about by John, falls into the 'structured' ritual category, the contents of the prayer are extemporaneous and serve as an example of the personal relevance of what is prayed about or prayed for. The prayer type described above and the contents thereof are rooted in the interviewees' context(s). As an example of this, at the time of conducting the interviewees, South Africa was experiencing a severe, nationwide drought. As a result of the drought many of the interviewees mentioned praying for rain, this was an element of their context(s) at the time. Andrew provides evidence to support the contextual nature of extemporaneous prayer by saying: "But there's nothing that I can say 'tomorrow I am [going to] pray about love, in an hours time I'm going to pray about faith' . . . it's how it happens in my life, you know, what things happen . . . " and: "I can't tell you that I have any days or any specific times something I'm going to pray about. It's what comes up in my life and what's happening . . ."

Rather than discussing abstract examples of the interviewees' accounts of their extemporaneous prayers, certain popular themes will be categorised and discussed instead. For example: prayer as thanksgiving or prayer as catharsis (as in the case of John that was quoted above).

2.3.2.1. Prayer as Thanksgiving

Many interviewees, when discussing what their prayers consisted of, mentioned giving thanks or being thankful. Mentioned previously were two examples of interviewees being thankful for waking up, for having breath, for being alive. These examples were mentioned as part of the relative interviewees' prayer rituals, describing their ritual processes. They also brought light to a theme that required reading and rereading the transcriptions. When searching for evidence of thanksgiving in prayers Simon made a transparent statement: "I think my prayers involve a lot of thanks rather than pleading and asking for things 'cause certainly, as a family, we've been very blessed . . . So we've got a lot to be grateful for." As will be discussed in a later theme, many interviewees describe requesting an assortment of things. Simon lays much importance on being grateful or thankful as his/

her entire answer to the question regarding what the interviewee prayers about was about thanksgiving "rather than pleading."

The importance of being thankful is explained by the interviewee, however further investigation into this as a theme was needed. It was discovered that six of the nine interviewees mentioned being thankful, in various forms, during prayer. Some of the interviewees' explanations of thanksgiving are broad, which allude to a more general attitude of thankfulness. Due to the contextual nature of extemporaneous prayers the context and content of thanksgiving are important aspects. Therefore what the interviewees are actually thankful for is paramount when seeking context.

First of all the evidence uncovered was Simon's contextual thanksgiving, quoted above. The second piece of evidence was provided by Peter, who not only uses the word 'thank' but also 'adore'. To adore is to love, the words are synonymous with the former being a more intense version of the latter. There is also an element of admiration when one adores someone or something. In order to understand the context, in this example, between 'thank' and 'adore' the following quotation from the interview with Peter is provided below:

> " . . . it's not because I sit down and say 'now I'm going to do adoration of Christ or God' . . . I'm all the time, while I'm driving; while I'm working; I can adore God because He's given me so much—there's so much for me to see in this world. Beautiful stuff and there's sad stuff but I still thank Him for whatever . . . "

Peter explains, explicitly, that he/she adores God because of what He has given him/her. Thus there is a strong link between the two terms mentioned above. He/she sees 'stuff', is thankful and therefore expresses adoration toward God. Within this example there is a clear link between adoration and thanksgiving and within this interviewee's context it is simple enough for him/her to adore God out of thanks. Behind both adoration and thanksgiving, in this context, are emotional undercurrents. To love or to adore is inherently emotional and for Peter it could be said that to adore, or express love, is done out of being thankful for feeling loved as a result of having "a beautiful home and having my [spouse] and being cared for." The context of Peter's thanksgiving is love and care, which in this explanation is reciprocated with adoration as a result of gratitude. Similarly to Peter's adoration, or admiration, related to thanksgiving is Phillip's thanksgiving involves admiration. Phillip begins his/her explanation of what he/she prays about, by saying: " . . . I pray to God to thank Him for His majesty."

While the terms 'love' or 'adore' are not used, there definitely is a sense of admiration.

The quotation above was the beginning of a comprehensive description of what the interviewee prays about. Included in his/her description was a list of giving thanks for various aspects of the interviewee's life and context. Phillip explained giving thanks for: "that I have seen or I have another day added to my life", "for all of the things that I'm able to do through Him", "for . . . His favour on my life and the life of my children", "for when I have a challenge and when I have issues that I can go to God and as true as true can be He comes through for me.", "for the small things and if it's big things I thank Him for the big things." and "for the favour; for the grace; for His mercy on our lives and for the things I want to do and I'm able to do." This answer was broad in the sense that Phillip described many different aspects of his/her own life that he/she is thankful for. The second part to the answer given by Phillip is as important as the first part, quoted and listed above. The interviewee goes on to explain exactly why he/she communicates all these thanks through prayer. The most peculiar point of his/her explanation is the interviewee's revealed perception of who or what God is to them. Phillip stated:

> "God is not only a doctor. God is everything that you want Him to be, so I don't only go to God for prayer for sickness. I don't only go to God for helping me with problems, I don't only go to God and say to Him: "God I want to do this, that and the other." I also go to God and I thank Him that I can thank Him."

This explanation could be seen as somewhat controversial in terms of "God is everything that you want Him to be . . . " However the focus here is placed more on: "God is not only a doctor." One of the research aims is to discover how people perceive God through prayer. Phillip provides a good example of just how God is perceived by people through their prayers. Generally speaking if one is ill, one would visit their doctor. In a similar sense when one prays for healing, be it from illness or any other physiological ailments, one (in this case Phillip) sees or perceives God as the proverbial doctor—available to cure or heal the proverbial patient. By Phillip saying that God is not only a doctor, he/she could be suggesting that in another scenario God could be seen or perceived in another role. This is most likely why the interviewee claims that "God is everything that you want Him to be, so I don't only go to God for prayer for sickness." Perhaps the word 'want' could be misleading and therefore the statement is not as controversial as it may seem, due to the interviewee attempting to explain that people can perceive God in a variety of roles depending on what is being prayed for/about.

Another perception that arose when examining the interview transcriptions came from John, who said: "I start my prayers with thanksgiving for the blessings and the things we have and praising God for who He is and the fact that . . . we are such small, insignificant people on this earth but He has the time for each and every one of us." Labelling this perception cannot be personified, however the Interviewee certainly perceives God as something much larger and more significant than any person.

By providing some of the examples given by the interviewees about thanksgiving and prayer, a discussion has begun and will be continued through interpretation in the next chapter. Phillip's explanation reveals at least one perception of God. This perception was mentioned as a result of the interviewee praying for healing and seeing God as a doctor. As a result of the perception of God as a doctor, by requesting healing through prayer, the next theme will be discussed below.

2.3.2.2. Prayer as Requesting

It became apparent, throughout the process of interviewing, that many of the interviewees spent much of their time praying on requesting. The thought behind examining and discussing prayer as requesting is that a variety of perceptions should come to the fore by discussing what interviewees requested through prayer. Much like the previous theme the answers given by the interviewees, on what they pray for or about, provide insight into their context(s) and the context(s) of their prayers.

A relatively straight forward example is that many of the interviews made requests, during prayer, for rain. The context behind this request is that there was a severe drought throughout South Africa at the time of conducting the interviews. The sub-contexts, in this example, are that the interviewees would be requesting rain for different reasons—or a combination of reasons. For example, many farmers were losing livestock due to a lack of water and therefore food supply as well as there being a more personal consequence of the drought in the form of water usage restrictions being imposed on households by the municipalities. In either example the sub-contexts are as a result of relevance to the interviewees, thus only a question remains: how is God seen or perceived in these prayers? While none of the interviewees explicitly mentioned why it was that they would pray for rain to fall over South Africa, the variety of sub-contexts can still be theorised, speculated and discussed within the overarching context of such a request. Of the nine interviewees, six mention praying for rain. The importance of these requests, in prayer, cannot be ignored as they serve as an indicator of the interviewees' larger context, a national consciousness, their South African context.

The relevance of this context is something that will be discussed in the next chapter, however there is no unique perception that arises when praying to God for rain. To find perceptions, it is necessary to focus more on the individual's context combined with the requests made—to investigate the context of individual and personal extemporaneous prayers. When asked 'what do you pray about?' Matthew mentioned praying for his/her business. Matthew explained that he/she prays for "guidance that the business is also furthering God's Kingdom—in the way that I do it and . . . the way that I act and, you know, react." Matthew did not explain what exactly his/her business is about, although praying for guidance for the way that he/she conducts hi/her business suggests that it is not important. Contextually, the interviewee is praying more for him/herself than for the business as he/she is praying for guidance in the form of his/her behavior and conduct rather than the prosperity of the business. In slight contradiction to the above, the interviewee did mention that he/she does pray for his/her business due to being unable to survive off his/her pension alone. Therefore there are two contextual aspects to the requests made through prayer for the interviewee's business.

The first aspect is that it would succeed for the interviewee to survive off the income and the second aspect is that the interviewee would be guided in the way in which he/she conducts him/herself resulting in the furthering of God's Kingdom. Within the context of requesting the success of the business, it could be speculated that the interviewee sees or perceives God, indirectly, as provider. The second context where the interviewee requests God to guide him/her in furthering God's Kingdom, suggests that the interviewee sees or perceives him/herself as a disciple. Although this perception is one of the interviewee's self rather than a perception of God, it points to a perceived relationship between the interviewee, as a disciple, and God. This perceived relationship will be discussed through interpretation in the next chapter.

Similarly to Matthew mentioning praying for guidance is James, who mentioned praying "for insight and wisdom in what I must do in a situation." Earlier it was explained that when Matthew prays for guidance, within his/her context he/she sees him/herself as a disciple. James's context is in no way similar, within his/ her context he/she is praying for insight and wisdom for the sake of enabling him/herself for a situation. Throughout James's interview, he/she was considerably unrevealing.

James's answers and descriptions barely scratch the surface to what was going on, however there were a series of hints made to a traumatic experience that the interviewee and his/her spouse had gone through. To ask God, in prayer, to provide insight and wisdom is to ask God to enable the interviewee. By asking God for these tools to enable him/herself, the interviewee sees or perceives God as an enabler or facilitator in the matter. James asks God to facilitate the situation by providing the interviewee with insight and wisdom, without which he/she would not be able to deal with the matter at hand. This is evident purely by the fact that the interviewee is asking for such tools for God to enable him/her "in what I must do in a situation." In comparison to the above Andrew prays "for some guidance for the day." While James's request alludes more to being enabled within a certain situation, Andrew's requests are more general and are more along the lines of assistance where and when it is needed. Overall the two examples are similar but are quite different when each example is explained. To enable someone could be explained as to provide someone with assistance where it is needed. While dwelling on the interview with John and Andrew, another perception of God comes from John. The interviewee described that he/she prays for "safe travels on the road - I mean Andrew drives a horrendous road every morning . . . " Within this context, the interviewee is requesting safe travel and by doing so is asking God to guard over or protect the person driving the "horrendous roads every morning." By requesting this it could be said that the interviewee sees or perceives God as a guardian—or God as a protector.

Lastly, for the interim, in John and Andrew's interview another perception was noted. When answering question two of the interview, Andrew said: "Listen, I need to talk to . . . uh . . . talk to You and I need to ask You, I need to . . . what's um . . . advice and I need counselling." Above terms and perceptions such as 'enabler' and 'facilitator' were used to describe how certain interviewee's see God through certain prayers within a certain context. Within this context, the wording lying in plain site, Andrew sees or perceives God as a counsellor who may be in a position to assist with a certain situation.

The final part of this section describes a number of examples and explanations provided by several of the interviewees. Throughout the interviews, the interviewees mention praying for other people. In general, if one was to pray for another person then one would be requesting something of God for that person in his/her context. The interviewee may apply their own context(s) to praying for other people as well. Of the seven interviewees that mention praying for people, at least three of them mention praying for loved ones whether it was "close family"(John), "extended family" (John), "kids" (Thomas), "other people" (Matthew and Peter), "someone" or "somebody (James and John), "sick people" (Phillip), "sick family member; the other group members; family members or friends" (James) or "one of my friends" (Andrew). All of the above examples are part and parcel of praying for other people. All of these examples involve requesting one thing or another for someone else and all of these requests pertain to the above given perceptions of God.

In review of this section, certain perceptions have been revealed. They are God as: doctor, provider, enabler or facilitator, guardian or protector and counsellor. In the sections that follow more perceptions shall be revealed through examining different examples of prayers, as stated by the interviewees. The above section is broad and will overlap with certain sections below, for example: James mentions requesting healing. Requesting healing is part of this section as a result of the healing being a request, however prayer as a form of healing is a different section which will be discussed below. The perceptions that were revealed above will be discussed in greater detail in the following chapter.

2.3.2.3. *Prayer as Healing*

The theme of prayers as healing technically falls into the theme above. This is because to pray for healing, whether for one's self or another person, is to request healing through prayer. James mentioned healing on two different accounts. The first quotation hints more at emotional healing , the second quotation is more explanatory and alludes more to physical healing—from sickness: (1) "Okay if I do pray, I will pray for someone to be healed; someone to be helped . . . But mostly about somebody who needs to be healed." and (2) "Well we discussed about people [who] need healing; you got a sick family member; the other group members; family members or friends." In both cases healing is being requested for other people, whether emotional or physical.

Phillip gave a similar example of praying for healing when he/she mentioned: " . . . we pray for sick people . . . " It could be argued that neither of the interviewees are praying, directly, for healing of the 'sick people' although indirectly by praying for the sick concern is shown for their health and most probably their return to full health. In both examples the explanations of praying for the sick are limited, there is a lot of room for assumptions. As with the 'definition', or lack thereof, of 'quiet time' when one worshipper mentions 'praying for the sick' to another worshipper—there would be a common understanding and nothing left to interpretation.

More directly, Phillip said the following: " . . . if I'm sick or whatever . . . um . . . I ask God for healing." This quotation demonstrates the common understanding that was referred to above and the possibility that on certain occasions, because of familiarity with the process of praying for the sick, mentioning that healing was requested would go unsaid. This explanation gains further proof by Jude mentioning: "I pray for people on the pew leaflet: the elderly, the sick, those in need of ongoing prayers." The element of care is implied, without which the interviewee would not be praying for such people. As care is implied so too are the requests for healing. Finally, further proof of this explanation is provided by Thomas, who said: " . . . at night, when I pray they're also in my prayers and then I will normally expand it to their jobs, which I either thank God for or, you know, the pressure they are under and that kind of thing; and then people that are sick or . . . in . . . in our other immediate circle or friends or friends of friends that you've been told about." Thomas feels it necessary to elaborate on what exactly he/she prays about when praying for "their jobs", however elaborates nothing when he/she mentions praying for "people that are sick." By using the above quotations and especially the similarities between them, there certainly is enough evidence to suggest that the interviewees imply praying for healing of the sick when they speak of praying for the sick.

In conclusion when considering the term 'pray for the sick', it should be considered that this term involves, and insinuates, praying for healing of the sick. This consideration applies to mentions of praying for the sick without the elaboration on the explanation involving mentioning requesting healing. Therefore whether healing is explicitly mentioned or not, when one prays for the sick one sees or perceives God as a healer or—in a more creative sense—doctor. Elements of the next theme have been discussed above in terms of praying for guidance. The next theme investigates prayers as a form of catharsis as well as the context in which these prayers are made and any perceptions they reveal.

2.3.2.4. Prayer as Catharsis

Matthew and Andrew both mentioned praying for guidance. By the interviewees requesting guidance or assistance they are admitting to needing help, the former with his/her discipleship through his/her business. The latter also explained praying for guidance and said the following: " . . . I need to . . . uh . . . talk to You (referring to God) and I need to ask You, I need to . . . advice and I need counselling." While needing advice can be seen as needing assistance or guidance, the interviewee also mentions needing counselling this could suggest a form of catharsis. Indirectly, by taking his/her problem to God in prayer and asking for advice and/or counselling, Andrew is releasing him/herself from the emotions that the issue, in need of resolution, has caused the interviewee to bear.

The proceeding theme discusses the idea of prayers as lament, examples will be provided under the next heading. Ideally, for the purposes of this research, the difference between prayer as lament and prayer as catharsis is that lament is expressing emotion about an issue whereas catharsis is purging the emotion caused by said issue thereby moving beyond lament. Catharsis, in this case, is then moving beyond the issue and the emotions attached and focusing on an outcome. This outcome may require, from the interviewee's perspective, assistance from God. An example of this can be seen in the following two segments from the interview with James: (1) when asked what the interviewee prays about he/she explained: "It will be like for myself, what do I do for this situation . . . " and (2) as part of the interviewee's explanation of his/her process of praying: " . . . I'm able to pray easily; pour my heart out to God . . . " By combining the two segments, within the context of the interview and James's emotional state, an example of catharsis can be seen. James pours his/her heart out to God and asks for assistance with a situation that he/she finds him/herself in. Contextually, the interviewee moves between releasing emotions to asking for guidance, hence the identification of catharsis and not lament.

At face value a client would approach a counsellor for therapy in a way which is congruent to the above explanation. By approaching a counsellor for therapy, the 'client' is admitting that assistance is required with an issue or situation with emotional purging—or catharsis—being part of the process. Therefore, in terms of the two examples given above, according to the interviewees God can also be seen or perceived as a counsellor. The following theme discusses a similar perception from a different emotional context.

2.3.2.5. Prayer as Lament

The difference between catharsis and lament, for the purpose of this research project, have been explained above. Lament is the expression of emotion without moving beyond the situation. Peter provides an example of the sort of lament that is understood for the purpose of this book:

> "I do expect because God promise[d] me, if I ask in His name He will grant me those answers but I know it's in His time. But I get very frustrated (interviewee laughs) at times like, you know, I'm praying desperately for our [child] in [The United Kingdom] who's just gone wayward and breaks my heart and . . . and God doesn't seem to be answering my prayer. But I know I mustn't stop because, as I said to you just now, in His time He will do things—when he knows the time is correct for Him."

In accordance with the explanation of catharsis, the interviewee is seeking an outcome to the situation described above. However this, so called, outcome is not materializing which stalls the interviewee in the heartbreaking, desperate and frustrating space that he/she describes in the excerpt above. It is appropriate that this 'lament' is in response to the sixth question which asked the interviewees whether they expect anything from prayer and what they expect. The interviewee's explanation of what he/she expects from prayer, in itself expresses a certain degree of lament with reference to him/her being frustrated by the lack of an outcome. More importantly is the impasse as a result of the lack of an outcome which leaves the interviewee in a constant state of lament, feeling heartbroken and desperate.

When answering the same question, John's answer is contrary to Peter's. Peter explained his/her answer using negative emotions that persist, while John said: "Um . . . for me it's . . . it's emotional. Um . . . emotional fulfilment because I've spoken to God. ., um . . . I've . . . I've laid my issues in front of Him." This example shows the releasing of emotions that is synonymous with catharsis and not the constant expressing of emotions that is consistent with lament—as portrayed by Peter.

In conclusion, there is a link between lament and catharsis. The former leading to the latter, depending on the opinion of the interviewee. What is meant by the previous sentence is that, to use Peter as an example, the lament being expressed is done in a hopeful way and when the time comes that there is an outcome to the situation, the interviewee will shift from lament to catharsis. In Peter's explanation there is said hope that his/her situation will change and when it does Peter will no longer have to experience the emotions associated with the situation. Rather he/she will progress to purging the emotions associated with his/her situation and therefore have experienced catharsis. In this example, the prospect is that the lament being expressed is part of the cathartic process—should the situation change in accordance with the interviewee's requests to God. Therefore it can be said that whether lament or catharsis, the interviewees involved see or perceive God as a counsellor or therapist.

The final theme for this section is of a somewhat familiar nature. Above and beyond all these perceived similes for God, the interviewees made countless statements that allude to God as God - the Almighty God that Christians go to church to worship. The aim of the above themes was to bring to the fore that Christians assume a lot more of God than simply an object of worship. With this in mind, it was important to show that worship and prayer are forms of communication used for many more reasons than simply worshipping, praising, submitting and confessing to God.

2.3.2.6. Prayer as Submission and Confession

As described in the themes above, prayer consists of more than simply submitting to God or praying for repentance. However, depending on one's understanding, submission and confession are default prayer settings. Without going into too much interpretation, as it is something that will be done at length in the next chapter, a good example of the default method of prayer as submission and repentance can be found in the regurgitation of the Lord's Prayer. Those that were interviewed from the Anglican denomination referred to the ACTS method of prayer. Peter gave a comprehensive explanation into what exactly this consists of, which is illustrated in the excerpt below:

"Um, you know the 'acts' for adoration, confession, thanksgiving and then supplication - I basically work on that but I mean it's not because I sit down and I say 'Now I'm just going to do adoration of Christ or God.' I, um . . . I'm all the time, while I'm driving; while I'm working; I can adore God because He's given me so much—there's so much for me to see in this world. Beautiful stuff and there's sad stuff but I still have to thank Him for whatever and um . . . confession obviously and then thanksgiving to me is for the everyday stuff that I've got and the beauty of having a home and having my [spouse] and being cared for. And then there's supplication—is really praying for other people and for my own family obviously, um, and I suppose for myself but that will come at the end . . ."

Of course this is an advised method of praying and in terms of this research, the content and context are what are of importance. This method provides a general view of what can be prayed about. This section, as titled above, considers prayer as submission and repentance. With regard to these two themes, Peter highlights submission in a subtle way by saying that he/she adores God also highlighting repentance by saying " . . . confession obviously . . ."

There were two interviewees that mentioned using the ACTS method of praying, however there are other examples of submission and confession, or repentance, throughout the interviews. One such example comes from John, who said: " . . . and praising God for who He is and that fact that, you know, we are such small; insignificant people on this earth but that He has the time for each and every one of us." By John saying that "we are such small; insignificant people", he/she is expressing that God is far larger and significant and that he/she expresses his/her submission through praise. Phillip, on many occasions, made references to God's majesty, sovereignty and grace. The terms majesty and sovereignty are used to describe God's stature as seen by Phillip. By saying " . . . I pray to God to thank Him for His majesty." Phillip is showing submission to God. This is done similarly when Phillip said: "In our worship . . . we . . . acknowledge God as a sovereign God, we acknowledge God for His majesty, we acknowledge God that all that we are and all that we accomplish and all that we do is only through the grace of God."

The interviewee, through acknowledging God's sovereignty and majesty, is explaining that he/she submits to God through prayer. The term grace falls under both submission and confession (or repentance). God's grace is associated to His majesty, which forms part of the submission element. However without the grace of God there is no repentance. Phillip's focus is more towards submission by saying that " . . . All that we do is only through the grace of God."

Thorough descriptions of the research findings from both the worship service observations and the interviews have been provided above. Before continuing on to the next chapter there is one last empirical description that should be done. Three of the interview questions pertained to the worship service. As a result of this it is necessary to describe the inferences the interviewees made when discussing the worship service(s) and, where necessary, compare the findings to the descriptions provided from the worship service observations. By broadly discussing matters that arose from the interviews and comparing them to the worship services across all three churches, a general consensus of the cultural 'wants' of the congregation(s) can be described. The description thereof will aid the research process when considering Chupungco's candle analogy, which illustrates the method of liturgical inculturation and liturgical interculturation.

2.4. WHAT IS GOING ON IN THE WORSHIP SERVICE?

Three of the eight interview questions were related to the worship service. The aims of asking each was to gain insight into the worship service appropriated by the interviewees. In order to keep this section as structured as possible, the content will be described in three sections—in accordance with the questions above. These questions were:

1. In general, what will prayers during the worship service consist of?
2. On a scale from one to ten, please plot your satisfaction with the worship service at your church. Please explain your answer.
3. In your opinion, should the worship service be adjusted so that worshippers could have better experiences of prayer?

2.4.1. Prayers During the Worship Service

The prayers during the worship service were observed by attending worship services at the three churches, they have been described in the thick descriptions in the appendices as well as in the comprehensive summaries provided earlier in this chapter. The importance here lies in the interpretation of these prayers from the interviewees' perspective(s). The answers given to question four should provide insight into how the interviewees interpret the prayers in the worship service. The first interpretation of these prayers is from Peter, who explains the following:

> "But very often, when they're doing the worship it's often asking for *Tanie Sarie se seer voet* (Aunty Sarie's sore foot) kind of thing, you know. And that, to me, is not worship that is asking for healing but, so . . . for me worship is adoring God, Christ, Holy Spirit and praising His name for what He's done for me and for all of us. So for me, I have a problem with that because I feel we don't do enough of the worship side."

Peter is quite clear in expressing his/her point of view that there is more praying for healing than there should be, according to the interviewee, and that there should be more prayers of adoration in the worship service. While there were prayers, in each church, for the healing of the sick they certainly did not appear to count for the majority of prayers during any of the worship services. It is clear though that Peter feels there should be less prayers requesting healing and more prayers of adoration combined with thanksgiving and submission—more praise and worship of God focussed prayers, rather than praying for people, their situations and needs. In comparison to Peter's concerns, Phillip explains—rather proudly—what the prayers during the worship service at the church he/she attends consist of:

> "In our worship, when we are together we . . . we . . . we . . . acknowledge God as a sovereign God, we acknowledge God for His majesty, we acknowledge God that all that we are and all that we accomplish and all that we do is only through the grace of God . . . And in worship it's just awesome that we can give God glory for: His favour, His blessings, His mercy, His grace. And for everything that we ask Him and when we worship it is a form of expressing our thankfulness to this great God."

Perhaps this is the worship or praise based prayer that Peter is seeking more of in his/her participation in a worship service. It should be mentioned that Peter and Phillip attend different churches, thus displaying the importance of the theory of a network society going forward into interpretation. This comparison will be interpreted along with many other situations, episodes and contexts in the following chapter.

The next comparison to be described is peculiar. Matthew and James decided to give answers that were more specific to their personal prayers in the worship service, rather than focussing on the liturgy. Matthew provided a lengthy explanation into his/her role in praying in the worship service. As it is a long winded explanation, some relevant quotes will be pointed out below:

- With regard to prayers before the worship service, Matthew explained: " . . . it has happened that the society steward hasn't pitched in time. Um, and then I will be asked to pray, you know, that it's not one of the officiants that's going to pray. And then, basically, that comes to mind . . . "

- With regard to praying for others during the worship service, the interviewee explained: " . . . pray with it—only when it is, when I really feel I should, will I go up and I'm with the people being prayed for, just to support them . . . and um, especially when not many other people are going up but I'm not going to be jumping up to . . . I've got to feel that I'm wanted there . . . "

On one brief occasion, the interviewee mentions that there are always prayers for the church. Matthew also mentions that there are prayers of confession. In both cases Matthew said: " . . . as the person is preaching you know . . . as they feel being led and I will just try and support them . . . if need be just whisper 'amen' or so—just quietly . . . " Matthew was concerned, mainly, with the contributions he/she could make to prayers during the worship service—explaining this rather than explaining what the prayers during the worship service consist of. In comparison, with Matthew who is more focussed on him/herself, James only explained the following: "Actually when I do seldom go to church, I will go more for the sermon and if there's communion I will pray for my situation at the rail . . . " Again, the interviewee is certainly focused on his/her prayers during the worship service and not the liturgy. This is fortified by James continuing his/her explanation with: " . . . otherwise I will go generally more for the service or the sermon and I don't always go, generally, to pray at church."

Contrary to these self involved prayers, John, Andrew and Thomas answered the question differently to those interviewees above. Each of them explained the prayers that were part of the liturgy, whether prescribed; planned or extemporaneous. Firstly, John explains the prayers one can expect in a worship service, at the church that he/she attends. Here are two quotations from the interviewee's response to the question:

> "... I think the prayers in the service are pretty ... uh ... fixed and, you know, they have prayers of thanksgiving, and prayers of intercession and so on."
>
> "... as I said: it's sort of for thanksgiving and for blessings and there's prayers of intercession and um ... if there's specific issues in the church, or happenings, or activities, or ministries that are needing prayer that will also come ... um ... you, you know ... it will be prayed about in the pulpit. Um ... collection has a specific prayer dedicated to that, after collection has been taken in."

John does well to summarize, generally, the prayers in the worship service. Prayers that are prescribed and could be part of the liturgy for his/her church come in the form of thanksgiving and intercessions. When the interviewee mentions prayers for specific issues such as happenings; activities or ministries, he/she is illuminating planned prayers and/or extemporaneous prayers. By mentioning that these prayers are prayed from the pulpit, the interviewee is placing the spotlight on those involved in the running of the worship service. Such as the minister, worship team leader and society steward. Thomas affirms what was said by John, when he/she said: "And then obviously the ministers or the society stewards or whoever will pray during the service ... um ... And you will often say your own little prayers as ... depending on what the sermon's about ... "

The reason why the prayers could be either, or both, planned and extemporaneous is because such prayers could be preplanned as part of the worship service—or extemporaneous. Interviewees John and Thomas shared no opinions on how they felt about this. Andrew, however, did have an opinion on these prayers:

> "I had a lot of fights about that, what's um, that you must have strict prayer for this, now this, and now we pray for this. To me, I feel, it has to be led by the Spirit and I feel sometimes we stop the Spirit, "Hold on you can't come into me now, I have to pray about ... " what's um ... "the offering now. You can't come into me now, I have to pray about this now." And I feel sometimes, we neglect ... what's um ... the Holy Spirit to take over the service or the ... um, the ... the worship at the time. Even with music, sometimes you can see that the church is really—the Spirit is there—the people are singing and there's really a vibe there, then all of a sudden because there is now certain things we have to do.

> Um . . . specifically, I call these, what's um, planned prayers—planned for this. I believe, I feel this has to be led by the Holy Spirit and I feel sometimes we're praying for things, what's um, unnecessary because of the rules and that's where I don't like the rules of church, you know. Um . . . I don't say it's wrong, what I just feel is . . . what's um . . . sometimes we neglect the Spirit to come and to talk to person on the pulpit's heart."

Andrew's opinion is important to this research process as it shows an example of someone whose cultural needs are conflicting with the traditions of the church. He/she even went as far as to say that he/she has had "a lot of fights about this." This opinion provides a platform for interpretation that will be done in the next chapter. In closing this section, Jude explains similarly to Interviewees John and Thomas by saying that:

> "Well we have a very set form: we kick off with praise, we do . . . after the introduction we do the gloria; then we move on and we do the penitence; then we move on from there and then there are the readings; then we do the creed; then there is the sermon; then there are formal prayers after the sermon; then there is the preparation of the gifts, which is the Eucharistic prayers; and then there are the concluding prayers."

Jude attends a different church to Interviewees John, Andrew and Thomas, thus showing that across the different churches and their liturgical traditions there are certain structured and planned prayers throughout the worship service. While the latter three, as well as Jude, shared no opinion on the matter, the opinion of Andrew shows that not everyone finds these structured prayers pleasing. Whether this is from a cultural affliction is something that remains to be discovered in the next chapter.

2.4.2. Satisfaction with the Worship Service

One of the interview questions asked for the interviewees to plot their satisfaction with the worship service on a scale of one to ten. While the numbers provided gave an indication of the interviewees' satisfaction, their explanations behind the numbers is of more importance. Their reasons for providing such a numerical rating out of ten are what is important. What pleases them and what doesn't is what is required for developing a new theory for praxis, after interpreting their reasons and explanations in the next chapter. During periods of reflecting on the answers provided by the interviewees, some valuable statements from Jude came to the fore. Before delving into describing the relevant data collected from the answers to question seven, it is important that perspective is gained into where the answers originated from. Illustrated below are quotations from Jude and his/her insight into why and how an interviewee would answer this question in a specific way—or from a specific point of view: Firstly, Jude mentions that: "What I get out of my church service depends on me and my attitude, my attitude to God, my allowing the Holy Spirit to operate in the service." Secondly, Jude shares that: "So I suppose it would be rating myself . . . " Followed by: "And so . . . for what it's worth, look one doesn't look at . . . at the church or at God, one looks at one's self rather."

These perspectives forced a paradigm shift: rather than focusing on what the church is or is not doing to satisfy the interviewee, it is important to rather consider the interviewee and not the church. The liturgy, and prayer liturgy, is the overall focus of this research project, however for this section of describing the data the interviewee is the research object and not the church and its liturgy. This question gave the interviewees the opportunity to commend the churches that they attend for worship services or complain about certain aspects of the worship service. Although, from the perspective of Jude, it also provided the interviewees with a time of introspection. Therefore allowing the interviewees to be critical of themselves in the worship service.

Throughout the interpretation of the empirical data in the proceeding chapter, specifically the data described below, it will remain imperative to consider and interpret the interviewees' context with regard to satisfaction. There is a participation element when developing a new theory for praxis, although the church plays a role in the satisfaction of its worshippers in the worship service the worshippers themselves play a role in being satisfied. A new theory for praxis has a liturgical element that should form part of the church's responsibility to its worshippers as well as a participant element where the worshippers have a responsibility to themselves and the church. This theory will be considered throughout the remainder of the research process: the worshippers exist because of the church and the church exists because of the worshippers. To borrow from the field of biology, after considering the perspective of Jude, there is a symbiotic relationship.

What is explained above, with the assistance of Jude, is that any given worshipper is as responsible as the church when it comes to their satisfaction with the worship service. If there were concerns shared by any of the interviewees, the majority thereof were adjustments the church could make to improve the interviewee's satisfaction, as worshipper, in the worship service. Few, if any, explained adjustments they could make—as worshippers—to improve their satisfaction therein. As an example of an interviewee explaining their satisfaction as a direct result of what the church was responsible for, is an answer given by James: "Okay, that would depend on who's preaching." The interviewee proceeded to explain that his/her satisfaction in the worship service is purely based on the homiletics of the preacher and more specifically the structure of the sermon. The ability of the preacher on duty to structure a sermon, is what is fundamentally key to James's satisfaction. To reiterate, James began his/her explanation by stating that his/her satisfaction is dependant on who is preaching. Matthew took a more pragmatic approach by offering his/her services in combination with a suggestion that he/she made to the relevant church authorities. The interviewee's explanation alludes to a concern, not only for increasing his/her chances for satisfaction in the worship service but also for others. Matthew stated the following:

> "Um, I have been routing, if that's the right word, for a prayer ministry and [one of the ministers] has been trying to accommodate this . . . You know, it's just been a matter of, you know . . . oh I'm [Matthew], you say you're [Interviewer] what can I pray for and then people say what they want and then the Holy Spirit just takes over."

Matthew does well to appropriate a role for him/herself in the worship service. His/her satisfaction is two-fold: on one side the interviewee is satisfied that he/she has a prayer ministry should he/she feel it necessary, on the other side the interviewee finds satisfaction in that he/she is able to be a part of this prayer ministry and enable others to find a similar level of satisfaction.

With regard to John similarities can be drawn to both Jude and James's perspectives. John begins by saying that: " . . . it really depends on what I would be looking for in a service . . . " This is similar to Jude's approach to satisfaction in the worship service. John then ends his/her explanation by saying that: "Sometimes I find the . . . the worship, the actual music . . . um . . . some of the mornings you'll go in there and I think "Wow, this is amazing . . . um . . . and I could sing for the whole service. And then other mornings . . . it's just not working . . . It drags and it's too much and I'm thinking to myself: "Okay, well how many more songs do I have to sing?"" This latter explanation takes a similar point of view to that of James. Interviewees Matthew and Thomas uncovered a variable that their worship service satisfaction was dependant on. Namely, the minister preaching at the worship service. Both have clearly been attending the churches they are at for decades and felt it necessary to list and compare ministers that either currently serve or have served at the churches in the past. To quote from their transcriptions is not necessary because of the subjectivity of the matter as well as the fact that their explanations were abstract. However, their points were made—that some ministers were more enjoyable to receive a sermon from than others, which played a role in the satisfaction, or dissatisfaction of the interviewees.

Finally, Phillip explained that his/her satisfaction is based on the development of the worship service and church community as well as the freedom to express him/herself without judgement from those around him/her. Below is an excerpt from Phillip's answer:

> "I would say nine. And the reason why I say nine is, if you look at our worship team there are new people that come on, you know, so that also expands. And um . . . but when we worship, I actually feel the presence of the Holy Spirit in our midst and the reason why I don't say ten is that in whatever we do we have to strive for better. So, I would say that one point that I didn't give them is like all the young ones that have come through . . . and, and . . . and all the ones that are practicing that they can also get to the place where the older ones are. But . . . but I love our worship, I love the praise. I love it because it makes me, it puts me like on a high. When I say on a high, I can sing and nobody will say to me "You're singing false" I can do my best and nobody can say to me "You're out of touch" I can . . . uh . . . I can clap hands, some people are whistling, some people do all sorts of things, some people jump around—that is how we worship God and I . . . I appreciate that. Because in our church, we all come from different homes; we all are at different levels of our worship; we all are at different levels of the journey, of our growth and our relationship with God but the most important thing—when we are there, we are there for a common purpose. And I love it, I love it."

Phillip is clearly impressed by the way in which the church joins the old with the new, encouraging anyone that wants to be a part of the worship band to get involved. From his/her explanation there seems to be a type of mentorship process for the worship band, where the younger worshippers are encouraged to practise and participate in order to be on a level that the current, older worshippers, are. Phillip also explained that: " . . . and I can say to you, I personally feel at home at my church. My children go to a different church, I feel at home - I am completely committed to my church. I get so much growth, spiritual growth; I get so much teaching and learning." By combining this with the interviewee saying that he/she is able to worship freely, without being told "You're singing false" for example, he/she is giving an example of the 'symbiosis' that was explained at the beginning of this subsection.

2.4.3. Perspectives on Adjustments to the Worship Service for Prayer

This subsection seeks to highlight relevant perspectives of the interviewees on how the worship service could be adjusted so that worshippers may have better experiences of prayer. As has become the norm, descriptions of explanations provided by the interviewees will be given in order to better understand what should be interpreted in the next chapter.

Matthew expressed that there should be more freedom, while in the worship service, to go to the rails and pray. He/she explained that: "You know, that you don't have to wait until right at the end when . . . uh . . . if you feel you want to come up . . . That's a moment but instead of sitting down, I must have the freedom to go to the rail. And then I believe the Holy Spirit will also call somebody to go up: 'May I pray with you?'" The interviewee explained this proposed adjustment in several different ways, each requiring the same adjustment: for the worshippers to have more freedom in expressing themselves. He/she concluded the explanation by saying: "One should not have to wait for . . . the opportunity presented by the minister. Sure, the Holy Spirit is working through him (or her) but I believe many people are touched and by the end, you know, they've sung the next hymn that—kind of—flame has subsided a bit." In summation, Matthew would appreciate the opportunity to go to the rails whenever he/she feels he/she should. Obviously this wish is for all in the worship service and not only the interviewee.

Peter explained that he/she would like to see more opportunities given 'open prayer'. The interviewee explained that: "I would like to see more of that because that does give the rest of the worshippers a chance to give their input." He/she further suggested that: "But it's got to be disciplined." Also explaining that 'free prayer' wouldn't work as it is too long. To summarise, Peter proposed that the church could spend less time on structured prayers that are prescribed by the liturgy and more time on 'open prayer'. Where the worshippers could pray extemporaneously rather than reciting a prayer from a prayer book or worship manual.

Interviewees John and Andrew agreed with each other that an adjustment could be made to the rigidity of the structured prayers. Below is an explanation provided by Andrew: "Exactly the same as the prayer, sometimes I can see how people, what's um, after prayer is really moved, you know, I see tears in the church. I feel, what's um, the minister is there now, he has to take it further. Um . . . and I don't see it because he's got now 'have to do this' and 'you have to do that' . . . " What they are suggesting is that the minister and worship team would adjust the worship service as it progressed by feeling the mood and needs of the worshippers rather than relying on and, so rigidly, following the liturgy.

2.5. CONCLUDING REMARKS

In closing, it appeared that Interviewees Jude and Phillip were content with the liturgical structures of their churches. While Simon and Thomas had nothing of relevance to add to the matter. Jude declined to answer the question directly and explained that worshippers will "go where they're fed." If they are not having worthwhile experiences of prayer "they're not being fed there and they're going to leave." Phillip answered the question by saying that it is not necessary to adjust the worship service so that worshippers would have better experiences of prayer. The interviewee said: "Well, I think . . . we do connect with God. I don't think that anything must change for us to connect with God more."

The next task of this process is to interpret this information using different sciences and theories. In terms of Osmer's four questions, the question "What is going on?' has been answered above through the descriptive-empirical task. The next task, the interpretive task, asks the question 'Why is this going on?'.

Chapter 3

INTERPRETING THE TALE
Why is This Happening?

THIS CHAPTER SEEKS TO gain understanding by asking a question, suggested by Osmer, "Why is this going on?"[1] This is the, so called, interpretative task. To best answer the question certain "episodes, situations or contexts", described in the previous chapter, should be examined through drawing on theories of the arts and sciences that will enable informed understanding and responses as to why these patterns and dynamics are occurring. This question is aligned with the research questions to seek understanding as to the main research problem: "how does the form and content of prayer impact the ways in which people connect with God and other people?" As well as: (1) how people communicate with God, (2) why people pray and (3) what people pray about. The latter three questions, as developed in the introduction to this book, should aid in better understanding that which is posed by the main research problem which is stated above.

The empirical data in the previous chapter has been categorized by episodes, situations and/or contexts, each of which will be interpreted through certain theories from determined arts and sciences. These arts and sciences and the relationship to the topic of prayer will form the sections below. Specific episodes, situations and contexts will be discussed under the appropriate headings. This research process is interdisciplinary and therefore in good practise, if an episode, situation or context is discussed

---

1. Osmer, *Practical Theology*, 4.

under one heading—through theory from one art or science—it should be discussed under each heading. As an example of this, when interpreting satisfaction in the worship service, it is important to not only interpret the relevant episodes, situations or contexts through theories from social sciences that align with Liturgical Studies but all of the relevant overarching theories from the arts and sciences. In essence, what should be seen below is interpretation through theories from the arts and sciences of: Liturgical Studies, Ritual Studies, psychology and sociology. These are the fields that have been drawn on for their contextual relevance to theology, as in a ritual-liturgical category, a liturgical-ritual category and a Pastoral Care category. It is within these contextual parameters that theories will be used, an example being that relative aspects of psychology and sociology will be drawn on within the scope of Pastoral Care. In certain instances interpretation through other ad hoc theories from relevant arts and sciences such as systematic theology and dogmatics will be used above, although, within the overarching arts and sciences of interpretation, listed above. The terms episodes, situations and contexts have been used several times in the above. These terms are defined by Osmer:

> An episode is an incident or event that emerges from the flow of everyday life and evokes attention and reflection . . . A situation is the broader and longer pattern of events, relationships and circumstances in which an episode occurs. It often is best understood in the form of a narrative in which a particular incident is located within a longer story . . . A context is composed of the social and natural systems in which a situation unfolds. A system is a network of interacting and interconnected parts that give rise to properties belonging to the whole, not to the parts.[2]

As an example of each of these terms, as well as the relationship between the three, that were found in the interview with Phillip. The interviewee begins one of his/her answers to an interview question by explaining that "In our worship, when we are together we . . . acknowledge God as a sovereign God, we acknowledge God for His majesty, we acknowledge God that all that we are and all that we accomplish and all that we do is only through the grace of God." This explains an episode as this is an incident or event. The situation, being the broader and longer pattern of events, is the worship service that the interviewee attends on a weekly basis. Therefore

---

2. Osmer, *Practical Theology*, 12.

the context would be the church system in which these situations, and episodes, occur.

Contexts, or systems, are a network of interacting and interconnected parts. Thus within a context there are microsystems and macrosystems. As an example of this, a macrosystem that forms part of a context is culture, while a microsystem is the church culture. Therefore as a brief explanation of this context's construction: the systems that are parts of this context include, but not limited to, the church system; the church culture and the cultures of the worshippers attending the worship service. As a result of this, contextual analysis is an important aspect of practical theological interpretation.

In order to properly analyze these episodes, situations and contexts it is important to consider all the appropriate theories from the arts and sciences that will best aid in developing an understanding for their occurrences. For this reason specific arts and sciences will be used to aid in answering the research questions. Some of these arts and sciences will aid in answering one of the research questions, while others aid in answering all three within the question associated with this task. As mentioned previously, each of the research questions was developed in order to aid the understanding of the research problem.

Within and outside of the church prayer can be seen as a ritual act, perhaps even a rite of passage, by examining the structures of prayers in comparison to ritual structures. Therefore it is necessary to interpret various episodes, situations and contexts through the lenses of Ritual Studies. The next section is dedicated to exactly that. It is important to remember at all times that this research is primarily from the field of Liturgical Studies and by drawing from other arts and sciences, therefore taking an interdisciplinary approach, the aim of doing so is only to benefit Liturgical Studies. The benefit of an interdisciplinary approach is it adds to already existing theories as well as developing new ones by borrowing and integrating theories from relevant arts and sciences.

3.1. RITUAL-LITURGICAL INTERPRETATIONS

First and foremost it is important to define the terms 'ritual', 'rite' and 'rite of passage', so that clearer insight into the nature of such prayer acts can be achieved through informed interpretation. Before defining, or considering definitions of, rituals an introduction to the topic should be given.

The aim of using theories from ritual and ritual-Liturgical Studies is to not only answer 'Why is this going on?' but to aid in answering the three research questions posed in the introduction . Therefore providing understanding as to how does the form and content of prayer impact the ways in which people connect with God and other people. "Human beings have been involved in ritual activities of some sort since the earliest hunting bands and tribal communities about which we have information."[3] In comparison to the extensive history of rituals throughout recorded human history, the study of rituals has only been in existence for the last two centuries. Ritual Studies is, thus, a relatively new science. By combining the two points made by Bell above, an agreement may be made that rituals are ubiquitous; that no society is without recognisable ritual. Contextually the church, and its worshippers, forms a society. This society is littered with an array of rituals, rites and rites of passage. Wepener, from a ritual-liturgical perspective, developed a working definition to explain the phenomenon of ritual:

> Rituals are often repeated, self-evident, symbolic actions, that are always interactive and corporeal, sometimes accompanied by texts and formulas, aimed at the transfer of values in the individual or the group, and of which the form and content are always culture, context and time bound, so that the involvement in the reality which is presented in the rituals remains dynamic.[4]

In addition to the above Grimes mentions that: "Ritual practices such as daily meditation and weekly worship are responses to recurring needs."[5] The reason for this additional description is to emphasise the importance of ritual acts being repetitive or recurring. Grimes added to this description with: "These rites move but do not transform." Prayer, within and outside of the worship service, aligns with the definition and description from a ritual perspective as it is repetitive, recurring and seldom transformational. It should be kept in mind at this point that a distinction should be made between ritual and routine—or repetitive or patterned behavior. On certain occasions prayer can be transformational, specifically when part of a rite of passage such as baptism. Below is a working definition of rites of passage , this is provided in the aim of excluding the prayers observed in the worship

---

3. Bell, *Ritual*, 1.
4. Wepener, *From Fast to Feast*, 36.
5. Grimes, *Deeply into the Bone*, 7.

Interpreting the Tale

services, as well as those described by the interviewees, from the category of rites of passage:

Rites of passage are the transportation of a person from one state of being to another. Effectively, a rite of passage will carry one from one state or place from which they are unable to return. Rites of passage depend on a 'momentous metamorphosis', not a moment where one gets emotionally carried away where after returning to their original condition. Rites of passage hinge on transformation and are developed with this in mind. Transformation can be explained as that moment in which a caterpillar becomes a butterfly, a moment after which one is never again the same. The aim being not only to transform the individual but also the community perpetuating the rite. Rites of passage differ to rituals, ritual practices such as weekly worship are responses to recurring needs. Such rites move people, rites of passage transform. Both, when enacted, involve performance but only rites of passage involve transformation.

Daily prayers, as described by the interviewees, as well as those in worship services can be excluded from the category of rites of passage in general. The aim of these prayers is not to transform, this does not subtract from their performances qualities. Rites of passage cannot, however, be completely excluded as there is one example that was observed in a worship service.

The observation of the third worship service at Hennops Methodist noted the baptism of five children. These baptisms and the prayers that were part of the rite of passage performance saw the transformation of the children being baptized as well as the transformation of the worshippers witnessing and participating in the rite. To summarize the transformation(s), the children were transformed in the sense that they are now members of the body of Christ (the church) and the worshippers are transformed in the sense that they are now accountable to those baptised and have additions to the body of Christ—to which they already, through baptism, belong. In this case specifically, the hope is that all involved would be transformed especially those baptised. Rites do not always achieve what they are designed to achieve, it is imperative that one not view such a rite from a beautifully romanticized yet fuzzy and subjective lens.

With the only account of rites of passage explained briefly above, the section below seeks to interpret ritual-liturgical prayers within the worship service(s). This is done by investigating recurring prayers or topics prayed for across the three churches, these prayers can then be interpreted by drawing on theories from the field of Ritual Studies.

3.1.1. Ritualized Prayers within the Worship Service

Each of these churches practise a different liturgy from the other, there are of course some observable similarities. The aim was never to develop three separate theories for praxis—one for each church. Rather the aim was to develop a single, suggested, theory for praxis that can be applied in different contexts—however with hermeneutical sensitivity. Therefore while certain rituals will be described from the context of the church from whence they came, they will all be interpreted through the lenses of Ritual Studies. Ideally, the outcome would be to interpret all rituals in a similar manner whilst comparing the rituals at one church to that at another. This will enable the development of one theory for praxis, which can be used as a starting point by all three churches. It is also important to mention the church from which the ritual comes, so that the context(s) can be taken into account along with the wider cultural contexts. By providing the context of the ritual, it aids in the process of understanding 'Why is this going on?'

An instrument, from the field of Ritual Studies, is available for this interpretive task, namely: "mapping of the ritual field."[6] This instrument explains the use of different ritual categories: "ritual space", "ritual objects", "ritual time", "ritual sound and language", "ritual identity", "ritual action" and "interpreting rites."[7] According to Swinkels and Post, Grimes' categories "are known in both anthropology and Liturgical Studies circles and they form the basis of almost all ethnographic instrumentation."[8]

Across the three churches, in observing three services at each church, a total of 77 prayers were observed. In order to steer clear of interpreting these prayers per worship service, within the specific churches context, groups of prayer types will be interpreted below. The aim of this is to interpret the types of prayers in a more generalised manner which will aid in developing a new theory for praxis. In certain instances contexts (or prayer types) will require situations and episodes, to aid in interpretation through explanations and discussions. In essence this means that there are two questions: the first being 'why is this going on within the church context?'

---

6. Grimes, *Beginnings in Ritual Studies*, 19.
7. Grimes, *Beginnings in Ritual Studies*, 20–32.
8. Swinkels and Post, *Beginnings in Ritual Studies according to Ronald Grimes*, 224.

Interpreting the Tale

which is general and sees all three churches as an example of a single church context, the second question is thus "why is this going on within a certain church's context?". The second question forms as a subquestion to the first, by answering this question it should provide better interpretation, where necessary, in answering the first question.

The first prayer type to be interpreted through Ritual Studies are the prayers ritualistically prayed in the worship service(s) that are prescribed by the 'worship manuals'. Examples include: praying for the blessing of the elements of the Eucharist, praying for the collection (otherwise known as offerings or tithes) and the Lord's Prayer.

3.1.1.1. Prescribed Prayers From the Worship Manuals

It was noticed in the participatory observations that there are many prayers per worship service, as mentioned above. These prayers included, but were not limited to, prescribed prayers that are dictated by worship manuals, prayer books or the order of service. These prayers are part and parcel of the liturgy of the church tradition—they are because the liturgy is. The prayers are found in certain liturgical literature that, for example in Smuts Anglican, can be found in the pews. For some worshippers, as observed in the participatory observations at Smuts Anglican with regard to the reciting of the Nicene Creed, these prayers are so familiar that they are regurgitated from memory, for others the prayers can be read aloud from the literature provided in the pews.

Ronald Grimes acknowledges that liturgy is one of the fundamental impulses of liturgy; he discusses that liturgy is a symbolic action in which a deep receptivity is cultivated.[9] Liturgical participants actively participate in a form of structured waiting, as they await what gives itself and what is beyond their control. However liturgy is not just a preparatory exercise or way of biding time but also the thing itself. The exercise of waiting is also the manifestation of the divine or sacred; especially in a sacred place or at a sacred occasion. This is otherwise known as hierophany, from the Greek word *heiros* meaning 'sacred' and *phainein* meaning 'to show'. Thus, in its broadest sense liturgy is the manifestation of the divine (God) in a sacred place. There is the possibility that prayer then epitomises this further by communicating with God (the divine). Using the explanation above, if liturgy is the exercise of hierophany then prayer supplements this manifestation

---

9. see Grimes, *Beginnings in Ritual Studies*, 43.

as those involved with the ritual act of praying are already in the belief that God is amongst them. Assumedly this is because one cannot talk to someone, or something, that is not in essence already present. Therefore prayer, as a liturgical ritual, supports the notion that the worshippers in a church are both awaiting the manifestation of God as well as realising that God has already manifested in the sacred place known as church.

The process of interpreting liturgical prayers through the lenses of Ritual Studies has begun above, initiated by describing liturgy as ritual. In general liturgical prayers within the participatory observed worship services often involved praying for matters such as: confession, praise, thanksgiving and supplication. As a conclusion to confession there is asking for forgiveness. As a conclusion to praise, requests could be made. Thanksgiving takes several forms, one of which is the thanksgiving for requests that have been fulfilled. Supplication is inherently the act of asking. Throughout the worship service there are prayers prescribed by the liturgy that are followed by the church. The majority of these prayers, with the exception of supplicatory prayers, involved moving to and fro between the prescribed concept (for example confession) and requesting (for example asking for forgiveness or grace). This narrative is what identifies liturgy as unique in terms of Ritual Studies because not only do worshippers communicate, proclaim and exclaim but they constantly ask.

Contradictory to statements made above, that there are prayers prescribed by the liturgy, Titans Church proves as an exception. It was noticed through the participatory observations of the worship services that there appears to be no set, rigid structure. However after observing and documenting three different worship services at this church, led by different people on each occasion, there was evidence of a certain, adopted structure. This structure serves as the liturgy for this church, although there is no comparable liturgical literature as can be found in the other two churches. As a result of this an informed assumption, through participatory observation, can be made that the worship service is so fluid that there is minimal distinction between ritualized prayers and the entire liturgy as ritual. Therefore, with the exception of certain prayers that will be interpreted below, there is no distinct ritualized prayer.

When considering the concept of ritualized prayer at Titans Church consideration should rather be on liturgy, or the worship service, as a ritual of which prayer is an element of it. To interpret prayers through Ritual Studies for the purpose of this research project is to see prayers as rituals within the worship service. From the context of Titans Church, this is not a plausible option as prayers are not generally announced and therefore cannot easily be differentiated from the liturgy as a ritual.

The majority of prayers observed at Titans Church formed part of the ebb and flow of the worship service, most often performed in between songs of worship. This majority were never announced, the prayers simply began between, or in the middle of, songs. The presupposition is therefore that for a prayer to be ritualized, it should serve as a separate occasion in the worship service and is begun by the announcing of the prayer—a ritual within a ritual so to speak. Therefore, as is the case with Titans Church, prayers that are not announced should not be deemed as separate rituals and are of a more extemporaneous nature. Extemporaneous in the sense that the norms of liturgical structure suggest that a prayer should be prayed between songs however the recurrence is not something that can be ritualized due to the episode(s) being repeated on a weekly basis without a recurring topic or even a general theme. This is not to say that such prayers are not of a ritual nature, they form part of the ritual process that is the liturgy. In such a context though, these prayers are not individual rituals as they form part of the receptive production of the liturgy, as a ritual, sometimes referred to as passion or deep receptivity.

Sufficed to mention, the ritualized prayers exude the same deep receptivity. The fundamental difference between ritualized prayers and the prayers described above is that the former serve as separate rituals within the liturgy—as a larger ritual. This separation can be identified by a call to prayer, such as "Let us pray." Although a more predominant factor of identification would be the prayer(s) as a listed item on the prescribed liturgy.

A discussion on ritualized prayer has begun above. This discussion will continue by drawing on theories of ritualization. Ritualized prayers have been described above with much focus being on the prayers prescribed by the liturgy—or liturgical tradition of the church(es) and their normative literature, should there be any available. The next section of this chapter aims to continue the discussion by interpreting the prescribed prayers through the theories of ritualization.

3.1.1.2. Ritualization

A description of the notion or ritualization is the intentional creating or inventing of rituals on the margins of existing rituals. To borrow from the field of Liturgical Studies and insert a comparison, it could be said that ritualization is to Ritual Studies what 'liturgy in the making', or *liturgia condenda* is to Liturgical Studies. This is to say that by taking a ritual and developing or inventing a 'new' ritual from it is similar to the re-invention of liturgy. In either case the re-invention is as a result of culture, inculturation and/or interculturation. In light of this it is proposed that ritualization, for the purposes of this research project, is part of liturgical inculturation and in these multicultural churches—interculturation.

Ritualization leads to the formation of rituals and therefore is presupposed in all other ritual modes such as liturgy. The term itself has been borrowed from ethologists, and/or biologists, Julian Huxley invented the term to explain the formalized activities of certain bird species.[10] Grimes' explanation bears significant understanding in this interpretive process:

> But even the most spiritualized monistic and dualistic religions depend on physical and biological processes in their representings and rememberings, in repeated liturgical seasons and rhythmic incantations. Moreover, even ritual-denying Protestant groups depend heavily on psychosomatically informed processes like "being moved", "feeling the spirit" or "having a full heart" . . . The history of the renewal of ritual action is the story of the eternal return to what are commonly specific ways. Ritualization drives humans in culturally specific ways.[11]

By considering the above there are some explanations to the question 'Why is this going on?'. First and most obviously in the case of Smuts Anglican where there are certain liturgically ritualized prayers that are used during certain parts of the liturgical year (or liturgical season). It was noted in the descriptions taken during the participatory observations at this church that there were certain ritualized prayers used during lent and after Easter. The necessity to examine when such prayers were ritualized is not of immediate importance to this chapter, the interpretation of their ritual inception is something that should be done in the proceeding chapter which involves the normative task. The importance on focussing on ritualization in this chapter, as part of interpreting by asking 'why is this going on?', is enforced by the last sentence of the excerpt above: "Ritualization drives humans in culturally specific ways." Seen as this project involves liturgical

---

10. see Grimes, *Beginnings in Ritual Studies*, 35; Miller-McLemore, *The Wiley-Blackwell Companion to Practical Theology*, 145.

11. Grimes, *Beginnings in Ritual Studies*, 35.

inculturation and seeks to reach an inculturated liturgy by developing a new theory for praxis, interpreting the relationship between culture and ritualization is the first point of departure.

Theoretical interpretation is the ability to draw on theory to understand and respond to particular episodes, situations, or contexts. The context in focus is that of ritualized prayers which can, for the purposes of this study, be defined as: weekly prayers that carry a theme and are prescribed by the liturgy of the church tradition, such as prayers for the collection, confession or repentance, thanksgiving and supplication. These prayers are neither episodes or situations, they are contexts within a system. In accordance with Osmer's explanation of what contexts are, namely a composition of social and natural systems, ritualized prayers form a ritual context within the larger context of worship. This is illustrated by the suggesting that worship does not necessarily include prayer—that is, a petition—although prayer often involves worship. By prayer involving worship, it suggests that prayer is a cause of worship, hence prayer is described as a sub-context within the context of worship. The process of drawing on theories from Ritual Studies has begun in the above, thus interpreting the context of ritualized prayer is in motion.

Culture, or cultures, is an integral aspect of the social system of the church. Therefore when interpreting the context of ritualized prayers within the context of the multicultural worship service, culture(s) cannot be excluded. Drawing on Chupungco's candle analogy, the first end of the candle—traditional—is, proverbially speaking, burning bright as a result of the main focus of the above discussions being on the formalized liturgy and the ritualized prayers contained within. Focus should as a result of this be turned to the other end of the candle—culture—to see where along the proverbial candle it meets with tradition. Firstly, by turning to the interviews, points were raised on the importance of rigid structures and timeframes placed on all aspects of the worship service. Andrew through a lengthy explanation did not seem to fully understand the need for such a rigid structure.

His/her interest in such prayers seemed bleak, situations such as this could be as a result of cultural aspects not fully understanding the tradition or said worship tradition not being 'relevant' to the culture of the worshipper(s). In such a situation, the processes of liturgical inculturation involve culture embracing—or critically rejecting—aspects of tradition and vice versa. The plural is used here because within the church a worshipper comprises of, or is influenced by, more than one culture, he/she has his/her heritage along with having adopted the culture of the church that he/she attends, for example. By explaining the frustration he/she feels for the rigidity of the worship service due to, but not only, ritualized prayers the interviewee is illustrating a lack of cultural comprehension of the church's tradition. Chupungco refers to this cultural aspect as 'wants', therefore it could be interpreted that Andrew's wants, as a result of culture(s), are not necessarily what is made available, or embraced, in terms of the ritualized prayers in the worship service. Therefore as a result of the interviewee's shared concerns, as a representative of the worshippers at his/her church, it is possible that the ritualized prayers (tradition) are not understood as a lack of liturgical inculturation and the rejection or embrace suggested by its, ought to be, critical-reciprocal interactions.

Peter shared a similar sentiment by explaining that there are various options for a certain ritualized prayer. He/she explained that for one of the ritualized prayers prescribed by the liturgy, he/she would prefer the use of "Form D" for this specific ritualized prayer instead of its more regularly used forms: "But we have four prayer options, so I feel we do the first and second and third—maybe not the third as much but the first two—the fourth one was open prayer and I believe we're not doing that at all and not enough." Peter seemingly has an understanding of the ritualized prayer (tradition) from the perspective of his/her culture.

Although through his/her explanation discusses and suggests that the culture (want) of the worshippers may meet the tradition of the church better, should this specific form of the ritualized prayer be used instead of its more frequently used alternatives. This provides an example of potential ritualization which, as explained above, is the "intentional development of rituals on the margins of existing rituals. In other words, ritualization could occur if the concerns of Peter were to be heard and considered by the church and his/her fellow worshippers, thus the ritual could in turn be developed with the intention of tradition embracing the culture, or 'wants', advocated by the worshipper. This serves as an example of tradition potentially embracing culture, while the example involving Andrew in the paragraph above is an example of culture potentially embracing tradition. There is also the potential for, in either case, tradition to critically reject these wants (culture) and vice versa, such is the process of liturgical inculturation—which can also be seen as the renewing of ritual actions, otherwise understood as ritualization.

In both accounts, the interviewees' concerns pertain not only to worship but communication with God and/or the Holy Spirit through worship as well as prayer. Among many references that indirectly discuss the interviewee's opinion to not end any communications that may be happening because of structural rigidity, Andrew stated the following:

> "You know, at one stage I thought of taking the offering totally out of the service because we are going huge . . . what's um . . . a worship and close to God and I feel it's here with us and all of a sudden stop and says: "Now we have to sit down and collect money." You know, ha . . . I just feel, what's um, it's . . . we break the Spirit there, we just . . . we took the moment away."

In this example the interviewee was referring to worship, although on several occasions Andrew also uses examples of prayer in the worship service while making reference to communication with, especially, the Holy Spirit—as illustrated in the example above. Both worship and prayer are acts of faith, both include an addressee: to worship or pray to God is to address God. To address someone, in this case the Holy Spirit or God, is to communicate with them. This address is explained by means of petitionary prayer, which presupposes a personal God with whom a relationship is established.

Different types of ritualized prayers reveal particular aspects of the relationship between God and worshipper(s). Revealing these aspects of said relationship aids in understanding 'Why is this going on?' As well as how the form and content of prayer impact the ways in which people connect with God and other people. Brümmer distinguished three different types of ritual prayer, each referring to different aspects of the relationship between God and worshipper. Firstly, petitionary prayers involve the establishment of a relationship between God and worshipper. Secondly, penitential prayers involve the repairing of the relationship, already established, between God and worshipper. Thirdly, thanksgiving prayers involve recognition of the relationship between God and worshipper.

In conclusion, these ritualized prayers, as a result of ritualization, have been intentionally developed by worshippers and the church alike in response to a realization of dependance on God. Such ritualized prayers invoke certain aspects of the relationship between God and worshipper(s). Therefore these prayers were ritualized in culturally specific ways as an exercise of 'hierophany'. Not only manifesting the 'sacred' but manifesting the relationship between the 'sacred' and the worshipper. Ideally the worshipper, through their culture(s) should nourish the relationship between him/herself and God through these ritualized prayers. As seen above, by providing examples of worshippers from the interviews, this is not always the case. Therefore not all of the ritualized prayers in the worship service are liturgically in(ter)culturated. This should aid in developing a new theory for praxis as it is not immediately important for this activity be named, however it is a more pressing matter to acknowledge that rites change; to see them as flowing processes and not rigid structures.

The proceeding subsection discusses various aspects of the above mentioned relationship between God and worshipper by interpreting specific ritual structures of prayer. Brümmer revealed aspects of the relationship between God and worshipper, however through qualitative and literary research these aspects have more depth than described above—especially through prayer.[12]

3.1.1.3. Ritual Structures of Prayer

Petitionary prayer involves an infinite spectrum of requests, for example praying for healing or receiving. Along with petitionary prayers are, as examples, penitential prayers; sacrificial or offering prayers and conversion prayers. Each of the above mentioned examples involve a tripartite structure. A more popular term for this is a threefold pattern or threefold scheme). These terms refer to the same concept developed by Arnold Van Gennep, who distinguished that rites are constructed of a pre-liminal phase, liminal phase and post-liminal phase.

According to Janssen, there is a clear structure to prayer, especially involving petitionary prayer: "There is a motive to prayer (a problem), an action to perform (ask something) and an effect to be sought (the solution [to] the problem)."[13] A comparison can be made between this ritual structure and the threefold pattern/scheme depicted to above. There is a sense of the pre-liminal (a problem), liminal (requesting through prayer) and post-liminal (a solution), when examining petitionary prayers. Throughout the participatory observations of all the worship services there were a series of petitionary prayers, many of which were described by the liturgies while others were of a more extemporaneous nature. As described and discussed in the previous section, the prayers prescribed by the liturgies can also be

---

12. see Brümmer, *What are we doing when we pray?*, 74.
13. Janssen, *The Structure and Variety of Prayer*, 31.

termed ritualized prayers. Below are a variety of examples illustrating the different relations between God and worshipper(s), as well as the relationship between worshippers as being church, through ritualized and petitionary prayers, using the threefold pattern involving liminality:

Table 2: Modes of prayer and the threefold pattern			
Mode of prayer:	Pre-liminal phase:	Liminal phase:	Post-liminal phase:
Sacrifice	Entrance	Sacrifice	Exit
Gifting	Give	Receive	Give back
Rites of passage	Separation	Transition	Incorporation
Confession	Guilt	Confession	Mercy
Healing	Sick	Conversion	Healing

It would appear, from the above, that there is a ritual structure to all prayers in the worship service—even the extemporaneous prayers. This ritual structure clearly involves the threefold pattern of liminality. With regard to petitionary prayers, the action of praying or requesting forms the liminal phase of the ritual structure. The same can be stated for confessional prayers, healing prayers, thanksgiving prayers and prayers of adoration. Each presumes a preconceived notion or state which is pre-liminal, proceeded by a prayer which is liminal, leading to an altered notion or state which is post-liminal.

The term liminality was traditionally used to describe a threshold, originating from the Latin word *limen*. Entering into prayer, from a ritual-liturgical perspective, is reaching a threshold—a gateway from one state to another. However these prayers, for the most part, are responses to recurring needs which is seemingly counter-intuitive to theory involving liminality and transformation. This, however, can be explained by using confessional prayers as an example: during the worship service one could feel guilty for sins committed during the week between the current worship service and one previously attended, therefore the worshipper participates in a confessionary prayer and is, in a post-liminal sense, moved by means of forgiveness. The same would occur at the next worship service where confessionary prayers would serve as the threshold to forgiveness, or as described above—mercy. This reiterates that these recurring rituals move but do not transform.

The ritual structure, described above, is not limited to prayer during the worship service. Many of the prayers in the worship are of an extemporaneous nature, whether performed by a member of the clergy or a worshipper in the congregation. As noticed in the interviews, there are an abundance of prayers performed outside the church by those that attend worship services. These prayers, too, involve ritual and—in some instances—the threefold structure described above. Liminality, as reaching a threshold, can transport individuals and groups through difficult circumstances by taking them from one phrase, for example grief, to a new phrase, for example closure. From the data gathered from the interviews, two themes arose namely: 'prayer as catharsis' and 'prayer as lament'. Both of these categories involve the emotional aspects, as illustrated by the following examples. James: "Um . . . because I seldom . . . pray alone, I actually find it very—not very—but fairly difficult to get into the discipline of praying alone but when I am able to, I'm able to pray easily; pour my heart out to God . . . "; John: " . . . for me it's . . . it's emotional. Um . . . emotional fulfilment because I've spoken to God . . . um . . . I've . . . I've laid my issues in front of Him."

In both of the examples the interviewees are illustrating prayer as having an effect on their emotions, as well as cathartically 'handing over' the worries or difficulties they have to God. Whether praying cathartically or communicating their difficulties in prayer, these interviews are realising a threshold in which prayer becomes a liminal phase. This notion presupposes another example of a threefold ritual structure, with catharsis (or lament) being the mode of prayer, thus moving from difficulty (pre-liminal); purging (liminal); to comfort (post-liminal). Such a mode of prayer is comparable to therapy, as a threshold, and the post-liminal comfort that is achieved upon completing one's therapy with a counsellor. The proceeding section of this interpretive chapter focusses on prayers outside of the worship service albeit it at home, in the car or at one's office.

3.1.2. "Quiet Time"

The above title was given to this section as an inference of the majority of interviewees explaining when their personal prayers occur. Of course, the interviewees did not only explain praying during their "quiet time" rather, for the majority, throughout the day—many of the interviewees reported praying either in the morning or the evening (usually whilst lying in bed), others reported praying during both of these times. This section seeks to understand, through interpretation, the personalised rituals that the interviewees have developed for when they pray in their own capacity outside of the worship service. In general there are times to these rituals ranging from the aforementioned "quiet time", praying on arrival at the office, praying whilst stuck in traffic to saying grace.

Drawing on theories from Ritual Studies to interpret "quiet time" and other personal prayer rituals—otherwise known as popular devotions—begins with definitions of rituals. It is important to mention that there is an aspect of community involved with rituals, which then forces the question: what role does community play in personalized rituals if the rituals are personal and/or private. Firstly, to say that these personalized rituals were invented by the person who performs them would be an uninformed and incorrect understanding. Secondly, when perusing literature on liturgy with regards to Ritual Studies there is seldom mention of the singular, as in 'person' for example, with references made more to plural forms or collective nouns.

While "quiet time" and other personalized prayer rituals are not typically liturgical as they occur outside of the worship service, under the presupposition that these personalized prayer rituals originated—or flow—from the liturgy, the relevant theories on rituals and liturgical-rituals that focus on the collective can be extended to include those people (or worshippers) that form part of such collectives (congregations) that perform their own prayer rituals in private.[14] As such, these private prayer rituals are otherwise referred to in the field of Liturgical Studies as 'popular devotions'.

The presupposition above is based on by the aphorism '*lex orandi, lex credendi, lex (con)vivendi*', adapted in the sense that the 'we' can be extended in exclusive circumstances such as "quiet time" to the 'I'. Along with the liturgical component is a cultural component, which also depicts an individual as part of a collective. Thus there is a sort of 'hereditary' process—from the worship service to the home, car or office, as seen where Matthew mentioned praying at home at "getting up time and going to bed time"; with Peter, the respective interviewee mentioned praying while driving and/or while working; with John and Andrew, where John described praying in the morning at home or while lying in bed in the evenings, while Andrew described a daily routine that involves praying once arriving at his/her office as well as 'talking to God' in the veld and praying while driving; in the interview with Simon and Thomas, where Simon mentioned praying in bed at night and Thomas refers to his/her quiet time in the morning;

---

14. Pecklers, *Worship*, 146.

Jude, where the interviewee mentioned praying in the morning and having a daily reading; with Phillip, wherein he/she explained that: "I pray every morning without fail; I pray every evening without fail."

Therefore what has been ritualized by the collective has been taken from the worship service and, when necessary, adapted for the individual. Ergo if the collective participate in thanksgiving prayers in the worship service then the individual will initiate one's own thanksgiving prayers in one's private capacity, in a similar ritualized manner to the example provided by the worship service—for example, 'we' give thanks in the worship service and 'I' give thanks at home. Take as example interviewees Peter and Jude, both describe a method of praying which they refer to as "ACTS." This method is suggested for worshippers to use in their private capacity. As an example of adaptation Jude said the following: "I'm not very good about praying for things for myself, I have introduced that. I think that I always thought it was a bit of a, a sort of an imposition if you put yourself first and kept praying for yourself."

This quote provides two examples of adaptation: firstly the interviewee adapted the "ACTS" method in the sense that he/she has "introduced" supplicatory prayers for him/herself which means, secondly, that he/she originally adapted the aforementioned method to excluded such supplicatory prayers. The example provided, while showing an example of adaption, also depicts an example of ritual re-invention. In general, the prayer liturgy at the Anglican Church attended by the interviewees takes on a similar method to "ACTS" in the worship service. Prayers of adoration (A) are proceeded, as the worship service continues, by prayers of confession (C), prayers of thanksgiving (T) and prayers of supplication (S). Thus providing evidence to support the claim that one's personalised prayer rituals are developed from prayer rituals in the worship service. How people pray, as asked by the fifth interview question, has begun to be explained by the interpretations above.

The interpretations above have been conducted by examining situations that were described by the interviewees, however these situations have concurrently been examined by looking at what the interviewees pray about. The reason behind this is because what people pray about influences and explains, to a certain extent, how they pray with regard to ritual language—terminology, articulation, linguistic styles, tone and formulae. Another example for interpretation is provided by Phillip, who described a variety of situations that aid in understanding the relationship between prayers in the worship service and prayers in one's private capacity. On several occasions the interviewee mentioned prayers of thanksgiving for God's sovereignty and majesty. When asked what the prayers in the worship service consist of, Phillip responded by explaining: "In our worship, when we are together we[. . .] acknowledge God as a sovereign God, we acknowledge God for His majesty . . . "

The aim of the research project was to develop a new theory for praxis that allows the congregation to connect with God in prayer and other worshippers through their cultural-liturgical and cultural-ritual contexts. As a precursor to this is the other research aim of this project, which seeks to determine if people can connect with God and fellow worshippers through prayer, within their diverse, cultural context(s). The example provided by Phillip sheds light on this. By praying on his/her own accord, in his/her private capacity, he/she connects with God through prayer. The importance of this research aim was to determine whether worshippers (in the form of interviewees) felt connected to God when they pray. However praying on one's own and connecting with God through prayer is one aspect of connection, the other aspect involving this connection is prayer in the worship service. Which is why Phillip's example is relevant. The connection that he/she feels when praying on his/her own is transferred to when he/she is involved in prayer within the worship service. While participating in the worship service Phillip feels connected to God but also to his/her fellow worshippers, this is evident by the use of the inclusive term 'we' and not the exclusive 'I'.

On the contrary interviewees Peter and Andrew describe having connections with God in the worship service, however they are limited by certain liturgical structural formalities which is something that concerns them. The concerns throughout their interviews, as partially detailed above, are expository dialogues between how they "talk" with/to God in their private capacity and how they lack the same connection, to complete satisfaction, within the worship service.

Peter attends one of the three churches that the research was conducted at, Andrew attends another of the churches and Phillip attends the third available option. Representatives from two of the three churches have concerns while the third representative is content. Which begs the question: what is happening at the third church that isn't happening at the other two? Answering this question should aid in developing a new suggested theory for praxis by considering theories on network culture. Theories on the network culture can be drawn from Liturgical Studies, which is the next lens of interpretation. With the appropriate theories of Ritual Studies used to interpret the ritual aspects of prayer being discussed above, the next step of this task is to interpret the relevant episodes, situations and contexts by drawing on theories from liturgical and liturgical-Ritual Studies.

3.2. LITURGICAL-RITUAL INTERPRETATIONS

The worship services at all three of the churches were guided by their relevant liturgies. These liturgies include prayer liturgies, which include ritualized prayers. As a result of the liturgies and their ritual components, the interpretations below will involve two lenses of interpretation: liturgical interpretation and, within it, liturgical-ritual interpretation. Within the worship service there are two prayer categories: (1) structured prayers which can be found in the worship manuals, examples include the Lord's Prayer; Eucharistic prayers and Baptism prayers, there are also (2) dynamic prayers which are otherwise referred to as extemporaneous prayers. The latter still form part of the liturgy as they are prescribed by it but only the topic, for example: praying for the collection or opening the worship service in prayer. The difference between the two categories is that the former involves word-for-word repetition, read from a worship manual or prayer book, while the latter involves unprepared prayers which result from a theme that should, according to the liturgy, be prayed about. With regard to the latter, the liturgy includes that which has become customary and not necessarily something that is dictated by a manual.

3.2.1. Prayer Liturgy

Interpretation through Liturgical Studies, and within it Liturgical-Ritual Studies, involves examining various episodes, situations and contexts for the possibility of liturgical inculturation or the lack thereof. This project also involved interviewing worshippers from a local congregation, a theme that arose from the interview findings was 'the power of prayer'. The concept of 'the power of prayer' was most often used to qualify a result—varying from a connection with God through prayer, healing through prayer or restoration through prayer . It could be that these results were achieved through, proverbially speaking, the cultural end of the candle and the traditional end of the candle both burning (in the worship service) and meeting in the middle—to use Chupungco's analogy once more. Prayers within the worship service are drawn from the tradition of the church, if the culture(s) of the worshipper(s) meet with this tradition then there is the possibility of prayer being 'powerful'. On the contrary, if the tradition and the culture(s) don't meet halfway then prayer could be mundane or hamper any results, should there be any from the worshippers' perspective, that were—or expected to be—in progress.

Considering, from an interdisciplinary perspective, an explanation of liturgy from Ritual Studies that Liturgy is a symbolic action in which a deep receptivity is cultivated. While also considering the concept of 'the power of prayer', connections can be made between this and the explanation of liturgy provided above. Namely between the 'deep receptivity', otherwise referred to as 'manifestation', and the abstract term—'power'. In emotive language, that which is powerful can also be referred to as deep, intense or meaningful. The responsibility of qualifying prayer as powerful or deep falls only on those experiencing it, through their culture(s), and not—instead—on the tradition of the church presupposing it. Therefore what needs to be considered when developing a new theory for praxis is the efficacy of the church tradition with regards to prayer in relation to the cultures of the worshippers.

Prayer occurs, as a ritual that is often repeated, interactive and symbolic action, within the worship service and is, essentially, petitioning God to descent during acts of worship, sometimes accompanied by texts such as a prayer book. If prayer is involved in the worship service, then prayer is also liturgical—the liturgy, or worship service, includes prayer as a ritual act. Therefore prayer is a liturgical-ritual act.

It was described earlier that a total of seventy-seven prayers were noted through the participatory observations across the three churches. Leading to an average of over eight prayers per worship service. This can be translated to the importance, for the worshippers, on said petitioning God to descent. In turn this raises two questions: (1) why is the liturgical-ritual act of prayer important to worshippers in the worship service? And (2) how is the petitioning of "God to come down" achieved or not? Both of these questions should aid in this interpretive task.

To best understand why prayer is important to the worshippers in the worship service, what should be interpreted are the situations and contexts in which episodes of prayer unfold. In order to develop an understanding of how prayer is enacted, certain episodes where events of prayer occur should be interpreted. As part of the interpretive task, both of the inquests described above will serve in understanding the question posed for this task—'Why is this going on?'. The first inquiry draws on theories from Liturgical Studies to best describe the phenomenon of prayer, which will be discussed below. The second inquiry, which also draws on theories from Liturgical Studies, is focused more on theories of ritualization as a result of the relationship between culture and church tradition.

3.2.1.1. *The Importance of Prayer from a Liturgical Perspective*

Hi In the descriptions above there are two theories that serve as an introduction to this section. The first was an explanation of liturgy from the perspective of Ritual Studies, which described the exercise of hierophany. The second explanation is from a liturgical perspective and is focussed more specifically on prayer, yet also refers to the manifestation, or to paraphrase the coming down, of God. Prayer includes requiring the infinite to become fixed; asking God to descent unto this world and time. All the while understanding that this expected presence can never be held as 'present-entity', however remains a 'trace of a passing always-already past'. Prayer is orientated toward the predominant eschatological nature of Christian faith and liturgical ritual.

This can be drawn in comparison to the explanation of liturgy as hierophany. This term refers to the manifestation of the divine or sacred (God), which can be compared to the petitioning of God to come down.[15] From either perspective, the act of manifesting or petitioning is done in expectation. Another important comparison is between the deep receptivity and the expected presence that can never be captured. In both accounts the worshippers are ready to receive God's presence—they are expectant. Therefore, in the context of prayer in the worship service, by engaging in prayer the worshippers are enacting God's expected presence. In other words they address God, by praying, in the expectation that God is there. It is clear that there is importance placed on the expected presence of God in the worship service and that it is enacted or manifested through the liturgical-ritual act of prayer.

By participating in the worship service, worshippers engage in symbolic actions and interactions that emulate that which has been envisioned of heaven through what has been learnt from the Gospels. Beginning his

---

15. cf. Barnard et al., *Worship in the network culture*, 359.

explanation on worship and society, Pecklers writes: "We speak of the 'already' and the 'not yet' as means of articulating that foretaste of heaven which we experience in worship even as we await the fulfilment of that heavenly vision."[16] What is of importance here is: " . . . as we await the fulfilment . . . " which implies a desire that is revealed through prayer, by "petitioning God to come down." Interpreting this desire will be focussed on in the next section which draws on theories from Pastoral Care—including theories from psychology and sociology.

In conclusion, the importance of prayer in the worship service lies in the expectation of worshippers to receive God into their presence as well as the desire to be in God's, heavenly, presence. Which in Ritual Studies terminology involves liminality. It has been described in a previous section that there is a ritual structure with regards to prayer—described as a threefold pattern. In the context of prayer in the worship service and its importance to worshippers, the threefold pattern can be described through its enactment: the pre-liminal phase is the 'desire', the liminal is the 'petitioning' and the post-liminal is the 'expected presence which can never be captured'. The evidence of a threefold ritual pattern leads to the second inquiry: how is the petitioning of God to come down enacted? The interpretation of which will draw on theories from Liturgical Studies that involve liturgical inculturation as a result of the ritualization of prayers in the worship service.

3.2.1.2. Liturgical Inculturation and Ritualization

The topic of ritualization has been discussed previously. Ritualization is culturally specific, rituals are re-invented and are dynamic—their form and content are always culture, context and time bound. By the term 'culturally specific', the understanding is that prayer, as Christian faith rituals, be enacted in such a way that it can be specifically understood by those enacting from their specific cultural perspectives. In other words that prayer traditions engage with cultural perspectives with the purpose of an effective ritual being enacted by those involved. The importance of prayer to worshippers in connection to their expectation of God 'coming down' should be of paramount importance to the enactment of the liturgical ritual of praying. Should prayer not be liturgically in(ter)culturated it would result in the worshippers being unable to properly enact the petitioning nor experience God's expected presence. This, in certain cases, may be made possible by

---

16. Pecklers, *Worship*, 163.

means of a counter-cultural approach which is to contextualise Christian worship including prayer, which necessarily challenges social injustices and transforms cultural patterns that focus on certain individuals or groups. Such is the case with Andrew 'wants' (culture) where, in the multicultural setting of his/her worship service, ritualization may come at the expense of others in the same worship service. Therefore, a counter-cultural approach could be beneficial in the sense that its intent is to transform all people and all cultures.

In lieu of the views expressed by Andrew, as well as those expressed by Peter, inculturation and/or ritualization could also approach such situations cross-culturally. Such an approach involves the sharing of elements of worship across cultures, an example of which can be found in the first participatory observation at Hennops Methodist where an African choir led the congregation in worship by singing the first two songs of the worship service and English and the third in an African vernacular. However, for this to be effective care should be taken that elements of worship from other cultures are understood and respected.

Ritual, in general, is essential to human life as it preserves cultural traditions and bridges periods of transition which lead to a change in the community. This explanation lends itself to two separate points of view. The first is that this explanation is more in reference to rituals in general, in other words cultural rituals as human activity. Secondly, it lends itself to an explanation of rituals within the church which infers that the term 'cultural traditions' can be replaced with 'church traditions'. The reason behind this alteration in terminology is because of the use of the word 'preserves'. The liturgy serves the church and its worshippers in preserving tradition, such as the Eucharist. The Eucharist is one of the sacraments, which have been of fundamental importance to Christianity and worship—especially the Eucharist, which can be traced back to the New Testament. Traditions should be preserved but it is equally important for these traditions to be understood culturally.

The importance and significance of liturgical inculturation, in relation to the statement made above that church traditions should be culturally understood, is because, according to Senn "every generation of Christians has been concerned that its worship be relevant, at least to them."[17] If prayer is relevant not only to a generation but also culture(s) then it is something that is understood by those present and participating. However, whilst

---

17. Senn, *Christian worship and its cultural setting*, 38.

considering generations, it was noticed that the older interviewees—in general—had no qualms with the liturgical-ritual structural formalities—in fact they rather enjoyed them. Some of the interviewees, those younger than the above mentioned interviewees, for reasons applicable to them had some disagreements with said structural formalities. These disagreements, as illustrated by Andrew and Peter are as a result of a lack of relevance—albeit it through critical-rejection or embrace—and/or understanding, in which case the church would do well to inform worshippers better or more thoroughly on why they preserve their traditions in such a liturgical way. Which would serve as a critical-reciprocal interaction between liturgy and culture. This will be considered when developing a new theory for praxis.

The inquiry that this subsection is based on asks how is the petitioning achieved or not. The summarised explanation is that whether the enacted petitioning is achieved or not lies in the relevance, or cultural understanding, of the liturgical-ritual act of prayer and then in the mystery of worship which can be developed through the inculturated involvement in the reality which is dynamically presented. The worshippers, and interviewees, do understand their contexts whether they are cultural or circumstantial because it is their own. Through this understanding they are able to enter into prayer either done in their private capacity or led by someone else or a group after an explanation of the context.

3.2.2. Liturgical Pastoral Care

In the previous chapter, which described and categorised the empirical data, various extemporaneous prayer themes were described. Some of which should be interpreted through the lenses of Pastoral Care, others should be interpreted from a liturgical-Pastoral Care perspective as they occur as part of the worship service. As an example of a connection, or similarities, between liturgy and Pastoral Care, van Ommen asserts the following:

> "The functions of healing, sustaining, guiding and reconciling are usually attributed to the practice of Pastoral Care. It might be helpful to think of our liturgies in these terms as well . . . Historically, the liturgy has been the primary means for Pastoral Care and so the four functions were carried out in liturgy. But even today it is not difficult to imagine how these functions work through liturgy. Liturgy sustains and guides individuals and communities; worship

services are places for reconciliation; the healing presence of Christ hovers in our worship services; through the Holy Spirit."[18]

In other words, van Ommen argues that the functions or Pastoral Care are already present in the worship service and the church as well as its worshippers would do well to become aware of this aspect of the worship service. van Ommen also brings to attention that the focus on this relationship between liturgy and Pastoral Care: that they are not the same, there is an interrelatedness and or polarity while not forgetting that the same applies to the relationships between liturgy and missions—for example.

It is the general assumption of lay people that Pastoral Care invariably refers to pastoral counselling, a one-on-one encounter involving one or other mode of psychological nature. Perhaps then there needs to be a shift in ideology from the worshippers perspective, one that notices that relationship between liturgy and Pastoral Care. Should this occur or already be in place, the worshippers would recognise the worship service as a time and place for healing, sustaining, guiding and reconciling. There is, however, ongoing development on the relationship between liturgy and Pastoral Care.

The aim was to develop a new theory for praxis which includes liturgical inculturation and within it—liturgical interculturation. There are those from a Pastoral Care perspective that are also concerned with liturgical renewal and the inculturation of liturgy. The concern appears not only where culture and tradition are considered but also the story of the Gospel within the liturgical tradition. In the above section, references were made to liturgical inculturation and the worshippers' need for relevance and understanding, here again there are concerns about the connection between the cultural story and liturgical tradition. One's cultural story is a form of how one understands the world they live in; how they reflect on such a world, the people they come into contact with and events that occur; how they measure themselves and how they 'write' their own story from the cultural story" they inherited.

In other words one's cultural contexts—something that has been referred to several times already. Secondly, the reference to the story of the Gospel could be explained, at least through the perspective of Liturgical Studies, as the important traditions such as the Eucharist which was briefly discussed earlier arose from the Gospels, in the Last Supper, and was evident elsewhere in the New Testament as a formalized tradition. This

18. van Ommen, *Liturgy and Pastoral Care*, 211–12.

tradition has been preserved and should be done so with considering the culture(s) of those participating in the ritual so that they may understand it and it would be relevant to them. In the development of a new theory for praxis consideration shall be laid on the relationship between liturgy and Pastoral Care as well as the affect of liturgy on Pastoral Care with regards to worshippers being able, through their cultural understanding and relevance, experience such functions—as the aforementioned—through liturgical rituals in the worship service.

Beyond the formalized liturgical rituals are such practices as prayer ministry, which was observed in two forms. The first was in the form of, what is popularly referred to as, an altar call. The second form that was observed at all three churches was done after the worship service, however still part of it. The reason for stating that this second form, here on out referred to as prayer ministry, is still part of the worship service is because it was in all cases advertised during the worship service. It may not serve directly as part of the formalized liturgy but was, in most cases, synonymous with the worship service. It can be best described as a voluntary aspect of the worship service and for the most part is done after the liturgical service as a matter of convenience: for the privacy of those in need of ministry as well as the consideration of those who are not involved's time.

It has been described above that the functions of direct, one-on-one, Pastoral Care are categorized as: healing, sustaining, guiding and reconciling. Considering this, there is the possibility that the worshipper seeking ministry requires more than that which is provided by the liturgy with regards to these categorized functions, such as James who seldom attends the worship service but regularly attends home group meetings who explained that: "Actually it's at home group that I probably pray the most", where most of the prayers involve praying for healing: "I'd say it's about 80, 90 percent is for healing prayer." It appears, from the account of Matthew, that prayer ministry is a component of the worship service that is more focused on the individual than the congregation as a collective. In addition to this, through the participatory observations at all three churches, it was noted that the respective clergy or lay person would announce or advertise that, to paraphrase, anyone in need of prayer should come to the front of the church after the service where they would be met by someone who has volunteered to pray with them. Thus allowing worshippers, as families, small groups or individuals, the opportunity for ministry in the form of prayer after the liturgy but still within the worship service.

Prayer ministry involves small groups, between two and five people, gathering around the altar or communion rails and engaging in prayer which usually involved the laying of hands—as was noticed in the participatory observations. As a result of not infringing on anyone's privacy, the content of the prayers is unknown however these encounters were often emotional for those who had gone forward in search of ministry. It is probably more applicable to apply a Pastoral Care narrative approach to liturgy here, due to the worshipper—he or she receiving prayer ministry—being able to share one's story, which up to that moment has been understood as a result of one's cultural story. As it is not involved in the liturgy, liturgical tradition need not apply nor be in relation to one's culture. This is not to say that Pastoral Care need not be considered throughout the liturgy, rather that prayer ministry is not liturgical by nature and is therefore an element of Pastoral Care included—by provision—within the worship service.

It is expected that prayers prayed during prayer ministry could concern similar matters to prayers that were described in the interviews. In the previous chapter different functions of extemporaneous prayers were described as prayer as: thanksgiving, requesting, healing, catharsis, lament as well as submission and confession. The final subsection of the liturgical-ritual interpretation will examine "quiet time" liturgy, which includes the extemporaneous prayer functions listed above.

3.2.3. Liturgical Pastoral Care

In a previous section, the ritual components of "quiet time" and other prayer rituals were discussed through ritual-liturgical lenses. The below are interpretations from a liturgical and liturgical-ritual perspective. These interpretations consider the concept of devotional literature such as The Upper Room. Devotional literature is a term given to Christian literature that serves as a guide for worshippers, seeking suggestions on how to further their faith. Furthering one's faith in this context ranges from learning how to pray for someone beginning a habit of "quiet time" or daily devotion, learning specific ways to engage in prayer related to certain topics, to finding ways to re-establish; deepen or differently experience prayer. Devotional literature is a concept that is not limited only to prayer, it also suggests topics to reflect on through meditation and/or learning certain behavioural techniques for one to practice throughout one's day-to-day live. Thus devotional literature possesses the possibility to affect, or suggest, the notion of *lex orandi, lex credendi, lex (con)vivendi* to the reader of such literature. There is a wide variety of devotional literature available however The Upper Room serves as a pop-culturally relevant example, it was mentioned in the interviews and falls into the scope of the network culture.

As the liturgy of the church is prescribed by the traditions of the church and the ritual acts that preserve them, so too the liturgy of "quiet time" is prescribed by the traditions of Christianity—as a behavioural aspect of living as Christ lived. In other words, through devotional practices one preserves the traditional modes of behaviour associated with devout Christianity, a constantly deepening desire to work toward peace and justice, as illustrated by Phillip: "And it is my prayer that . . . um . . . when I talk to people, I don't only say this about God but they would actually see in how I conduct my life . . . um . . . that I am a Christ follower." Examples of this include praying, meditating and behaving in a manner which would agree with the commandment: "Love one another. As I have loved you, so you must love one another" (John 13:34 NIV) as well as: "Do to others as you would have them do to you" (Luke 6:31 NIV). This describes once more the aphorism *lex orandi, lex credendi, lex (con)vivendi*. Specific content aside, it can be hypothesised that in general devotional literature, in a similar manner to the liturgy, aims at maintaining certain traditions. The discretion and discernment of such literature rests on the worshipper and their culture. In other words one will make use of devotional literature they find appropriate to them through one's relevance to it and understanding of it in conjunction with their liturgical traditions.

Not all the interviewees, or worshippers, make use of devotional literature. Some have developed their own procedures for "quiet time" and praying in their private capacity, which was discussed in the previous lens of interpretation. To answer 'why is this going on?' it is suggested that such a daily ritual is in response to a recurring need—the need felt by a worshipper to communicate with God.

Such a daily ritual is congruent with the septuple rhythm, that is the relationship between that which is done or experienced during the week and the liturgy in the worship service, for which there are two different points of view—the Catholic and the Reformed. One point of view is that the lived experience is jointly indispensable with the contemplative life culminating in a complete Christian existence. The other point of view is that work, liturgy, labour and worship must all complement each other. Whether it is perceived that the worship service, and the liturgy contained within it, is at the beginning of the week or the end of it what is important to this explanation is that which is done on Monday through to Saturday is a reflection and/or continuation of that which is experienced on Sunday in the worship service. The liturgy of a Sunday worship service extends into the week or is the conclusive responses of gratitude and adoration at the end of the week. From either point of view there is a relationship between one's daily rituals, such as "quiet time" and the worship service. One's day-to-day life events (*lex (con)vivendi*) effect the way in which the worship service is experienced (*lex orandi*) and the worship service affects the way in which one experiences day-to-day life events. If and when needed devotional literature aids this rhythm.

3.3. INTERPRETATION THROUGH PASTORAL CARE

Pastoral Care is not limited to any specific methods, practices or techniques, rather it demonstrates various responses of a person or people inspired by God's love for another or others. The interpretations discussed below consider psychological and sociological theories within the scope of Pastoral Care. One of the research questions was: why do people pray? This question was asked with the aim of understanding the reasoning and motivation for praying, which was best answered by considering psychological and sociological points of view.

3.3.1. Prayer as a Phenomenon

One of the reasons for including both psychological and sociological views of prayer, within Pastoral Care, is because prayer is both personal (private) and communal (public). As noticed in the participatory observations and the interviews people, exclusively, pray alone—whether in the worship service or in their private capacity as can be seen in the thick descriptions of the participatory observations as well as in interviews: Matthew; Peter; John and Andrew; Simon and Thomas; Jude and Phillip. These same people also, inclusively, pray in groups: as a family, in a cell group or in the worship service, which was also noted in the participatory observations conducted at Titans Church for example. Whether publicly or in private in certain episodes, situations and contexts people feel the need to pray. Another of the research questions is: what do people pray about? This second question aids in answering the first, playing a causal role in understanding the motive behind praying. Traumatic experiences are an unavoidable part of human life. As and when these experiences occur many people find it appropriate to share their thoughts and feelings on these matters with other people, which has been termed a disclosure process. By praying about such experiences and communicating one's thoughts and feelings through prayer may serve as a disclosure process to God. This could certainly be one explanation of a specific reason for praying, however not all prayers stem from a traumatic experience. The motive for praying described above is something that provokes attention from a Pastoral Care perspective. Pastoral Care concerns itself with traumatic experiences and the wellbeing of those experiencing them. Of the functions of extemporaneous prayer listed from the interviews the majority are related to difficult or traumatic experiences, these are: healing, catharsis, lament and submission and confession. Each of these has the potential to involve a disclosure process, especially catharsis and lament. It was explained in the previous chapter that both of these functions involve sharing emotions, the former serves in purging emotions associated with an experience while the latter serves simply to express such emotions.

From either a private or public perspective sharing, expressing or purging thoughts, feelings or emotions on difficult or traumatic experiences is a disclosure process. These prayers and the associated functions of a disclosure process could be helpful to those praying. Similarly to one sharing thoughts and feelings with a close friend, family member or confidant. Which, potentially, gives an explanation as to why one would find it helpful to adopt a disclosure process when praying about difficult or traumatic experiences. By sharing whether with another person or by means of prayer, one is communicating. Christian prayer is intimate communication with a benevolent God, categorized into two types of prayer: verbal and mystical (or contemplative) prayer. The former can be subdivided into categories such as: petition, intercession, thanksgiving and adoration. The latter can be explained as giving one's full attention to relating to God in a passive, open and nonverbal way. An added explanation of contemplative prayer is to wait on God to deepen confidence in His power and love thereby growing in Christlikeness. Up to this point what has been referred to as meditation can also be termed contemplative prayer.

From the point of view that prayer is a communicative—communicating with God for a purpose, in terms of the research question 'why do people pray?'—a sociological study's findings revealed that prayer is not simply a ritual; rather it is an action that participants believe has an impact on their lives. Thus far, from the interpretations of psychology and sociology the following can be provided as a working definition of prayer: as a phenomenon, prayer is communicative ritual. The purpose of communicating, or the motivation behind prayer, is that it has an impact on the one praying. Prayer is an intimate form of communication, whether verbal or contemplative. The phenomenon of prayer can also be explained as an expression of need and/or an affirmation of faith. The discussion above has alluded to prayer as a form of expressing one's needs by means of petitioning or a disclosure process that concludes with an improvement of one's well-being whilst or after enduring difficult or traumatic experiences. Prayers as affirmation of faith were observed in the participatory observations of the worship services.

Under the informed assumption that the theories from psychology regarding prayer can be applied to situations such as the worship service, what applies to the 'I' also applies to the 'us'. In other words by combining psychological theories on prayer with comparable theories from sociology, it can be determined that theories applicable to the self are also applicable to the selves in the worship service. Therefore it can be theorized in developing a new theory for praxis that when worshippers—as a collection of selves—are gathered together in the worship service, liturgical tradition should meet culture to allow communication with God in relation to impulsive, disclosure process, intimate or petitionary prayers that allow worshippers to pour out their hearts—in a cathartic manner. It is assumed, due to lack of data as a result of privacy, that the same would occur in situations of prayer ministry.

In conclusion, a working definition on the phenomenon of prayer from a psychological, sociological Pastoral Care perspective is provided. This working definition is an update on the one provided above, as a result of further insight and interpretation:

As a phenomenon, prayer is a communicative ritual. Prayer communicates expressions of need and affirmations of faith. Expressions of need can be communicated through prayer in expectation of improving one's wellbeing—or self. In such cases prayer is as a response to a need. The motivation for, or purpose of praying, is that it has an impact on the one praying and/or being prayed for. Christian prayer is an intimate form of communication, whether verbal or contemplative, with a benevolent and loving God.

Interpreting the Tale

In concluding this chapter it is necessary to mention that insight and understanding, through the process of interpretation of certain episodes; situations and contexts, has been gained. This aids in developing a new theory for praxis, in which it is important to consider the discussions above involving the ritual, liturgical and Pastoral Care aspects and contributions to prayer in the worship service. The insight gained through the above descriptions and discussions has been achieved with regard to the research problem. Therefore aiding in better understanding how the form and content prayer impact the ways in which people connect with God and other people. Throughout the process of interpretation, the relationship between church tradition and culture has constantly remained in consideration. The reason being that the aim of a new suggested theory for praxis is to form an inculturated liturgy.

The core insights that have been gained in this chapter involve: certain similarities between liturgical inculturation and ritualization; the nature of personal prayer rituals and popular devotion; the phenomenon of prayer from the perspective of Pastoral Care which included theories from the fields Psychology and Sociology and led to a working definition of the phenomenon of prayer. The interpretation of certain episodes, situations and contexts from the fields of Liturgical Studies, Ritual Studies and Pastoral Care led to better understanding and further insight into the ritual structures of different modes of prayer, the relationship between the worship service and "quiet time" and the importance of prayer from a liturgical perspective.

Chapter 4

Learning from Good Practice

The previous chapter focused on specific episodes; situations and especially contexts, drawing on theories from the arts and sciences to interpret them. This chapter seeks to interpret certain episodes, situations and contexts—gained from the empirical data—using theological concepts, some of which have already been introduced in the previous chapter, such as theories from the fields of Liturgical Studies and Pastoral Care—thus constructing ethical norms to aid in developing a suggested new theory for praxis, whilst learning from good practice. In light of this study involving theories from Ritual Studies, the interpretation of episodes, situations and contexts using theological concepts should be done in conjunction with using concepts and definitions from Ritual Studies. The aim of doing this is to consider the ethical norms and good practice from a Ritual Studies perspective and ritual-liturgical perspective. As with the previous two chapters and their respective tasks, this chapter also has a pertinent question: 'What ought to be going on?' Normative interpretation examines that which derives from certain standards or norms, hence the question proposed in connection with this task of practical theological interpretation.

The normative interpretations below begin with theological concepts, first and foremost from systematic theology. The normative task of practical theological interpretation should not be confused with traditional disciplines such as systematic theology. The reason for including systematic theological concepts in this study is to provide theological substantiation for the concept/notion/idea of 'church' and with regard to the research question of this study, the theological basis of the relationship between unity and diversity and the implications thereof for 'being church' in the twenty-first century. This is also a relevant example of the interdisciplinary nature of this study, the basis of this primarily liturgical study is an aphoristic concept used in systematic theology: *lex orandi, lex credendi, lex (con)vivendi*. This chapter is sectioned by using the three individual aspects of this concept.

4.1. KEY CONCEPTS FROM WITHIN THE FIELD OF SYSTEMATIC THEOLOGY

As mentioned above, the beginnings of the normative task consider theories involving ecclesiology, especially concerning literature on unity and diversity. The reason for this point of departure is in light of the cultural diversity in South Africa, as depicted in the introduction to this book, as well as the research aim which seeks to determine how the form and content of prayer impact the ways in which people connect with God and other people.

Recognising that the research was carried out across three different liturgical traditions, in one city, it is important to consider that these three churches—as the church—show a sense of unity in their liturgical practices throughout their liturgical diversity. The church father, Irenaeus, envisioned a liturgical or ritual unity within a liturgical diversity. The reason behind mentioning this is due to the acceptance that the liturgical traditions at different churches differ from one another, but also show similarities. With regard to this study and the traditions and churches that were studied, none of the three are 'wrong' in their liturgical ways and as a result there are grounds for acceptance of the other's liturgical interpretations, which are rooted in their traditions. Thus there is an element of 'unity' amongst them through their common liturgical practices, although there is also liturgical diversity. The interpretations below are focused more on 'what ought to be going on' within a church in relation to the diversity of worshippers in attendance.

The problem of the church with regard to inclusivity and exclusivity has been a problem since the time of the early proclaiming of the Gospel by the apostles. Three millennia later and this problem is more complex and even more intense. From the viewpoint of Western culture, the issue of unity and diversity is closely linked to concepts of linearity, spatiality and binarity. This serves as a connection to what has been discussed above and what will be discussed in the subsection below. These brief introductory remarks lay the foundation on which to ask 'what ought to be going on?'

4.1.1. An Ecclesiological Perspective

The notion of complexity in the above quotation is not only alluding to the inclusivity, exclusivity, unity and diversity of cultures in the church. This complexity refers also to other forms of diversity, such as race, gender, gender identity, sexual orientation and age. Each and all of these components add to the complexity and intensity of the problem regarding the relationship—or tension between—inclusivity and exclusivity. While the magnitude of this problem is something of concern to systematic theology, for the purposes of this study the focus shall be placed on cultural diversity and the 'problem' regarding inclusivity. In the field of systematic theology, current research utilises Trinitarian theology to approach the tension between unity and diversity, or between identity and otherness, with regard to inclusivity when it comes to 'being church'. Whilst considering this problem along with relative ethical norms and good practice, while also considering the aim of developing a new theory for praxis, it is important to consider 'church' in binary terms of visible/invisible. The 'visible' church is understood as the phenomenon of church apparent in the present. Whereas the 'invisible' church refers more to the church already as one because of the mutual belief in God. In the 'visible' church, as it is in the present, church unity cannot be seen as a reality 'now' purely because of the diversity of humanity. However, looking at the 'invisible' church, church unity need not be realised 'now' as all believers are invisibly 'one'. This provides a space for homogenizing and heterogenizing because achieving unity in the midst of 'otherness' is seen as an insurmountable task.

From a practical theological perspective, "the 'visible' church" can be equated to 'what is going on' while "the 'invisible' church" can be seen as the 'what ought to be going on'. The latter referring to that which should be the ethical norm(s)—or good practice—in an ideal world where the earthly (visible) church becomes the heavenly (invisible) church. The notion expressed above is, thus, the 'visible' church is that which Christians physically attend while the 'invisible' church is the hopeful ideal that is sought to be achieved. There is yet another way to consider this concept: the 'visible' church as the human version of the 'invisible' church, which is divine.

The argument that is made above, referring to the realization of unity being currently unachievable, is a presupposition that shall be considered as part of developing a suggested theory for praxis. The reason being that, through considering 'what is going on' and 'what ought to be going on', one is investigating the present episodes; situations and contexts while considering future episodes; situations and contexts. In other words, examining the present in comparison to ethical ideals and good practice, whilst developing a new theory for praxis as an ongoing result of this process—or recurring re-invention. It is important to mention that homogenizing and heterogenizing is referred to when discussing unity and diversity within the church and not unity of the church. Thus referring to the relationship(s) between human beings, encompassed by a desired relationship with God. In other words, being concerned with seeking the visible unity of Christians and not (necessarily) of the church.

The visible unity of Christians in the worship service could, supposedly, be achieved through the inculturation (homogenizing) and interculturation (heterogenizing) of the liturgy. From an ecclesiological perspective, the Pauline concept of the church as the body of Christ is relevant. Beyond the idea that if the church is the body of Christ, and Christ is its head, meaning that the church would be nothing without Christ, is the specification that there is one body. While considering this concept of the church is the body of Christ and Christ is the head, it is possible that the body functions harmoniously—that, so called, 'body parts' are not in conflict with one another. In other words, a body needs both legs to work cooperatively in order to walk for example. To take this imagery further, within the body are many parts—or cultures—and each part has its own cells, the cells of the lungs being different to the cells of the heart. However the heart and lungs function in harmony to oxygenate blood and pump it around the body, the heart deals with 'the otherness' of the lungs to function in unison as one body. Similarly, within a multicultural church, the cultures of those participating in the worship service should deal with each others' 'otherness' in such a way that there is homogenous and heterogenous unity in the worship service. Scripture reaffirms this fundamental, albeit profound, need for community: "The eye cannot say to the hand, 'I have no need of you,' nor again the head to the feet, 'I have no need of you'" (1 Cor 12:21).

An example of the proposed dealing with otherness, with the aim of unity, can be seen in the first participatory observation at Hennops Methodist, where the participants of that worship service were led in worship by a traditional African choir. Such a way of worshipping is not the norm, however the choir did well to adjust itself to the songs of worship and hymns that are not culturally theirs. From the worshippers' perspective, those in the congregation did not do well to adjust themselves from the norm—to sing in the unusual manner produced by the choir. It was noted in the thick descriptions for this participatory observation that in general the worshippers appeared to find the choir difficult to follow. From a liturgical-ecclesiological perspective, this is an example of the diversity and unity—or lack thereof—in the worship service. Each of these cultures, the traditional choir and those who could follow as well as those who found it difficult to follow, experience and interpret the traditions of worship differently. As a result there is a struggle in dealing with 'the otherness'. This struggle was noticed especially when the choir led the congregation into worshipping through the singing of a song in an African vernacular, as was noted in the first participatory observation at Hennops Methodist Church.

The concept of unity in the church, from a cultural perspective is something that is concerned with fellowship by means of liturgical inculturation and liturgical interculturation. The section below discusses the theological concept of *koinonia* from a systematic-ecclesiological perspective. It is important to be reminded here that when referring to liturgical inculturation, prayer and one's connectedness to God and fellow worshippers is the main concern. This is as a result of the first research aim, which seeks to determine if people can connect with God and fellow worshippers through prayer, within their diverse, cultural context(s).

4.1.2. *Koinonia* and *lex (con)vivendi*

The term koinonia, which refers to 'communion' or 'fellowship', possesses both vertical and horizontal aspects. The former refers to the relationship between believer and God, whilst the latter to the relationship between individual believers. The importance of *koinonia* and or *lex (con)vivendi* is very simply conveyed by Thiselton: "If a person was not part of a community of God's people "in Christ", that individual would hardly be "Christian"!"[1] This illustrates the importance of the horizontal aspect. In terms of the vertical aspect there is an understanding that lies at the heart of Christian theology, that Christians' most basic need is communion with God. Prayer adds both aspects of *koinonia* by its expressions of the longing of another's

---

1. Thiselton, *Systematic Theology*, 311.

heart in intercessory prayer; and by giving an honest and vulnerable expression of the heart's longing prayer connects people with God and to all needs fulfilled in Him. With regards to determining if people connect with God and fellow worshippers through prayer, the above are ecclesiological examples of 'what ought to be going on' in terms of 'being church'. Both quotations also serve as expressions of the notion of *lex orandi, lex credendi, lex (con)vivendi*. However, this is not necessarily what is always going on, as pointed out by Andrew in the previous chapter for example. Considering the above excerpts as good practice, they allude to both 'what ought to be going on' as well as literary evidence that aids in determining if people can connect with God and fellow worshippers through prayer.

In the section above a discussion began, from an ecclesiological perspective, on the topic unity and diversity. Included in this discussion was the comparative relationship between inclusivity and exclusivity. This discussion and the relationships, mentioned above, included within are concerned with the "horizontal aspects" of *koinonia*. The horizontal component of koinonia refers to the fellowship, communion or relationships between believers. In a multicultural context the notion or inclusivity and exclusivity is relevant, as described by Volf: "Much like Jews and Muslims, Christians can never be first of all Asians or Americans, Croatians, Russians, or Tutsis, and then Christians. At the very core of Christian identity lies an all-encompassing change of loyalty, from a given culture with its gods to the God of all cultures"[2]. The excerpt, above, is taken from a section in his book "Exclusion and embrace", which Volf titled "Departing . . . ", which begins with an analogy of Abraham departing his comfort zone in being faithful. In understanding this analogy and the excerpt above, Volf is suggesting that one's culture should be secondary to one's faith, whether Jewish; Muslim or Christian. This understanding alludes to an example of inclusivity and exclusivity within horizontal koinonia: by declaring one's faith one is inclusively part of the fellowship of believers, while inherently being raised from a culture and declaring one's faith from such a perspective one is exclusive, different, an 'other' in fellowship with 'others'. By being the 'other' is inherent of being oneself, in other words because of the complex matrix of factors—or identity—that defines an individual, the personhood of one is 'otherness' to other individuals and vice versa. The cultures and uniqueness of individuals should not be ignored in inclusive

---

2. Volf, *Exclusion and embrace*, 40.

fellowship, or worship; being in *koinonia* does not mean downplaying or ignoring the distinctive personhood of each person.

Up to this point the focus has been on the fellowship between believers, the discussion continues by making references to the 'horizontal line' of *koinonia*. Firstly, some explanations are required: on either end of the horizontal line are the 'believer', associated with each term are the aspects of the two relationships described above. On the one side, are the terms 'unity' and 'inclusivity' which depict half of the components concerned with the relationships that both influence and describe horizontal *koinonia*. On the other side, are the correlating terms that oppose those on the first mentioned end of the same line.

The horizontal line serves a larger purpose than that which is described above. The line should be pictured to be pushing either end of an elliptical shape, the one side—inclusivity—pushes, or oppose, the other and so the other— exclusivity—opposes the one. Metaphorically, they oppose one another in the same manner that polar opposite ends of two magnets repel one another. Simply, inclusivity is the opposite of exclusivity and within this a tension is created which is why there should be an elliptical shape and not a circle. When describing relationships between human beings there are constant comparisons made between the 'I' and the 'we'. The concept of *ubuntu* serves as further indication of the complexity of inclusivity and exclusivity, or unity and diversity. *Ubuntu* is a well known phrase, colloquially translated as "I am because we are." Even as a philosophical ideal, within the translated statement, there is still inclusivity and exclusivity. By stating that: "I am because we are" the 'I' is declaring itself as exclusive, whilst also realizing its inclusivity within the 'we'. In a similar manner the hypothetical believer becomes, inclusively, connected with other believers and God by joining in prayer—as described above. However, said believer could remain exclusive by praying in honest, vulnerable expression of one's own heart's longing. In the event that one believer's expressions of his/her heart's longing are different to those of other believers, then said believer becomes exclusive within the worship service.

Along the horizontal line, and intertwined with the tension between inclusivity and exclusivity, is where liturgical inculturation takes its place. From the discussions above it could be said, from an ecclesiological perspective, that liturgical in(ter)culturation seeks to aid the exclusive (culture) in becoming inclusive within the worship service. The importance of this is that fellowship (*koinonia*) is not simple social exchanges with one another in a church building but common participation (*lex (con)vivendi*) as one who, as a member of the body, holds a joint share in the body of Christ. At this point it is important to remember that when referring to culture, the description thereof goes beyond one's heritage or ancestry but includes such aspects as: financial status, race, gender, sexual orientation and any other factors that contribute to the complexity that makes one unique. The complex matrix of factors, which there are an infinite possibility of, could enhance one's exclusivity within the worship service and *koinonia*. One's exclusivity cannot be avoided although their inclusivity, or faith, in the worship service should be paramount.

The two subsections above focus mainly on the concept of being church (*lex (con)vivendi*) with particular attention placed on unity and inclusivity. As mentioned in the introduction, there is causal interrelationship, albeit complex, between prayer, belief and living together (or being church)—as the one affects the other(s). As an example of this interrelationship is the community of believers providing an important environment for parameters in hearing the voice of God; where the subjectivity of faith is embedded in the community of faith. Whilst considering this interrelationship, and after discussing ecclesiological ideals and norms of being church—living together in a faith community, it would be prudent to shift the focus to theories on belief.

4.1.3. Lex Credendi

The focus shifts here from being church (*lex (con)vivendi*) to belief (*lex credendi*), however due to the interrelationship it is worthwhile to discuss one in terms of the other. One can experience his/her own life as a life of fellowship with God, experience the sensory world as an expression of God's glory and grace, and experience of worldly events as: good and acknowledged as being of God's intentions, or bad which is acknowledged as contrary to God's will. In essence this denotes that religious experience is hermeneutical in the sense that it involved interpretation of ordinary and mentionable experiences of the comprehensive lived experience.

It is convenient that the term *lex credendi* falls between *lex orandi* and *lex (con)vivendi*. Mentioned above is that faith, or belief, is a hermeneutical process of interpreting living (*lex (con)vivendi*) and religious experiences, of which prayer could be included. Therefore, beliefs are influenced by life experiences and religious experiences, while beliefs simultaneously affect the way life and worship are experienced as believers claim that their interpretation is true. Thus as one experiences living (*lex vivendi*), so through hermeneutics they believe (*lex credendi*) and as one experiences worship (*lex orandi*), so through hermeneutics they believe (*lex credendi*). Thus, through faith one interprets life hermeneutically and develops certain beliefs. These beliefs should then relate the meaning of life experiences to God, which should be the norm for believers.

The final subsection of ecclesiology steers the focus from the 'being church' and 'belief' aspects of the aforementioned interrelationship, to the component involving worship or prayer. It is imperative to consider all three components of this interrelationship whilst the focus is more towards discussing the lex orandi component, which is where this discussion continues below.

4.1.4. *Lex Orandi*

The discussions above have provided insight into the ideals and norms of being church and belief. This subsection focuses on worship, prayer and their function in *lex orandi, lex credendi, lex (con)vivendi*. It was mentioned in the previous chapter, that liturgy as a ritual is in a preparatory exercise and a way of biding valued time; but it is not just preparatory but also the thing itself. Likewise, spirituality is the practice of one's fellowship with God but it is not merely practising. As one practices their fellowship (*lex orandi*), so they enact their beliefs (*lex credendi*) and so they live (*lex vivendi*) and participate in being church (*lex (con)vivendi*). This does not necessarily to worship or prayer but the liturgy as a whole, including all forms of spirituality. Through prayer believers realise various aspects of living in fellowship. In other words, the above serves as an example of *lex orandi, lex credendi, lex (con)vivendi*. This was of importance to the investigation of how the form and content of prayer impacts the ways in which people connect with God and other people.

Another interpretation of the interrelationship between living, believing and praying is in that through prayer people express their worldly experiences. These expressions are attitudes that are embedded in emotions, volitions and knowledge. All of this is shaped by experiences and the interactions therein with the world and other people. During prayer this experience is brought into focus in a personal and subjective manner; through prayer people express to God their lives and faith as they experience it.

Importantly, there is then a case of: 'as we live (together)' and experience the world and life, 'so we believe' through feelings, moods and thoughts, 'so we pray'.

This chapter seeks to interpret certain episodes, situations and contexts using theological concepts—thus constructing ethical norms to aid in developing a suggested new theory for praxis, whilst learning from good practice by asking the question 'what ought to be going on?' As such the content above involves discussions and descriptions of ecclesiological ideals and norms. In some cases the 'norms' may seem unobtainable, hence the inclusion of the term 'ideals' which is relative to answering the question that Osmer has associated with the normative task. Therefore, the sections above consider norms and ideals from the field of Ecclesiology, whilst keeping in mind that lessons can be learnt from 'good practice'. In terms of liturgical inculturation and liturgical interculturation, lessons can also be learnt on what 'good practice' is from an ecclesiological point of view. An explanation was given above on how liturgical in(ter)culturation finds its place between the tensions of inclusivity and exclusivity, unity and diversity, which is part of 'being church'. Remembering that, in the city of Centurion, being church involves multiple cultures and their wants to be inclusive in 'being church'. By gaining insights into 'good practice' and learning from it, the liturgical traditions of the churches involved could be better equipped to interact with the (multi)cultural 'wants' of worshippers. The next section of this chapter considers relevant perspectives from the combined fields of liturgical and Ritual Studies to aid in understanding what ought to be going on.

4.2. A NORMATIVE LITURGICAL-RITUAL APPROACH

In the previous chapter, which focused on the interpretive task, similarities were drawn between the concepts of liturgical inculturation and ritualization. *Liturgia condenda* as well as liturgical inculturation and ritualization, are all continual or ongoing processes. For this reason, the above concepts have been grouped together and will be compared for their similarities. This exercise is conducted with the aim of gaining insight into what ought to be going on with regard to liturgical inculturation and its ritual influences.

It is of importance to mention that both liturgical inculturation and ritualization are concerned with the cultural influences on tradition. In other words both concepts focus on the relationship between cultural and its effects on making tradition (worship) relevant to the current generation and vice versa. Another similarity that should be remembered is that prayer, as included in liturgy, is inherently ritual. As a point of departure it is imperative to acknowledge the similarities between liturgy and rituals; rituals change, they are flowing processes and not rigid structures; while within liturgy there is liturgical inculturation with is a continuous process. It should be mentioned that one of the aims of liturgical inculturation is inclusivity in terms of cultural relevance to the traditions of the worship service—or liturgy. Thus this section is concerned with how the form and content of prayer impact the ways in which people connect with God and other people from a normative liturgical-ritual perspective.

In terms of learning from good practise an example that can be scrutinised from the perspective of liturgical inculturation, or ritualization, is the ritual act of baptism that was noted in the third participatory observation at Hennops Methodist Church. If correctly performed this ritual, which is a rite of passage, will achieve that which it was designed to achieve. A critical factor in its achievement lies in the inculturation of the rite of passage. If the baptism ceremony is culturally relevant to the worshippers then only will transformation have taken place. It should be noted that this discussion is a hypothetical and not a criticism of the actual ritual that was observed.

As mentioned in the previous chapter, that which was observed and documented was intended to be a ritual of inclusion through transformation. If this transformation was achieved then both those being baptized and those witnessing the baptism were all inclusive of being church. It should be mentioned that not all of the five children or babies have the same culture. This raises the question: by making the decision to have their children baptized, are all the parents of the notion that the liturgical aspects of baptism are inculturated and that ritualization has occurred in terms of the traditional ritual of baptism? This question can be, hypothetically, answered with regard to 'what ought to be going on' by drawing on theories involving liturgical inculturation and ritualization. The hypothetical norm will firstly be described from the perspective of liturgical inculturation, in the subsection below. These descriptions will be followed by describing the same norm from the perspective of ritualization. Following the descriptions mentioned above, a discussion can be had by comparing the two approaches.

4.2.1. Liturgical Inculturation

In the previous chapters, descriptions of the concept of liturgical inculturation were provided. Liturgical inculturation is an ageless concept that has been termed or labelled more recently. There is a reciprocal relationship between tradition and culture that results in a new entity. Ideally tradition is absorbed into culture and culture is fully understood by tradition. The result is that a people would be able to experience a tradition, in this case baptism, as their own cultural event because said people would be able to identity their own language and ritual forms in this new, culturally relevant, tradition. In other words the liturgy, or baptism, remains traditional however it is also a new tradition due to the causes of culture. Therefore, in answering the question hypothetical from a normative perspective, the tradition—baptism—is what it always was but is new in the sense that it has been culturally adapted for the sake of it being culturally understood.

To 'answer' this question further it could be suggested that the parents, from the various cultural backgrounds, experienced their own baptismal rites of passage as a result of them being able to connect with what was going on, inclusively and exclusively, due to cultural and traditional assimilation. It should be mentioned that this is a hypothetical due to this discussion simultaneously investigating what ought to be going on. To ask 'what ought to be going on?' is to consider not only norms but ideals; as such there is an understanding that inculturation is not unilateral, it must involve reciprocity and a mutual respect between tradition and culture, and that authentic inculturation respects the process of transculturation. This means that the liturgy as tradition and culture are able to evolve through mutual give and take without the one infringing on the other. This continual evolution between culture and tradition can go wrong, this happens when the critical balance is tilted more towards one of the components than the other. For this reason the analogy provided by Chunpungco is used when describing liturgical inculturation. It is understood that if both ends of the candle are burning simultaneously that they would meet in the middle of the candle, which alludes to proper balance. There is one vital action that is imperative to this process, namely discernment; continuous discernment and even discerning discernment. Through discernment the evolution, liturgical inculturation, is both tradition being absorbed by culture and tradition absorbing culture—or the former critically rejecting the latter or vice versa. As part of discerning there are questions that should be asked of tradition and culture from the perspective of the other.

Therefore, a conclusion can be drawn thus far, namely that liturgical inculturation is not culture conforming to liturgical tradition neither should tradition be warped and thereby conform to culture. Hence liturgical inculturation is a balanced, reciprocal relationship based on critical discernment between culture and tradition. To answer, in terms of 'what ought to be going on?', the hypothetical norm would be that those experiencing the rite of passage, the baptism, are connected to it; can identify with it and are transformed by it due to the tradition being absorbed by their culture and vice versa. In this normative hypothetical which describes what ought to be going on, the liturgical tradition—in this case baptism—is not imposing itself on the culture(s) of those experiencing and performing the rite.

As proposed above, the section below will consider this hypothetical from the perspective of Ritual Studies by discussing the concept of ritualization from a normative approach. In the previous chapter the term ritualization was described and certain elements thereof were discussed. The subsection below continues this discussion with the aim of concluding this section by comparing the concepts of liturgical inculturation, discussed above, with ritualization.

4.2.2. Ritualization

In parallel with that which has been descriptions above, this subsection will continue using the baptism noted in the participatory observation as a hypothetical, 'what-if', to describe what ought to be going on. In the previous chapter an explanation of ritualization was provided, mainly that it leads to the formation of rituals. Ritualization can also, and has been in the previous chapter, be described as developing or inventing rituals on the margins of existing rituals.

Ritual is best viewed as a process, not as an enduring system or set of types. Rituals do not simply happen, they are enacted—performed—as responses to social dramas. The processes of rituals are developed through ritualization. The following excerpt should also be considered, in explaining the importance or relevance of ritualization[3]:

> Coming together and pushing apart—intimacy and aggression, symbiosis and isolation—are some of the most basic rhythms

---

3. Grimes, *Beginnings in Ritual Studies*, 35.

from which ritualization is constructed; hence, these actions are quite susceptible to habituation. Rites should not fail to deal with the systole and diastole of human action, but often they do. The result is habituation, the freezing of action. An unfortunate tendency of Western theories of ritual is to define ritual as if it were habituated behavior. But habituation is the bane of ritualization. It is imposed in the form of ought-filled, unmindful heteronomy, which is then hidden from view, denied. So authentic... ritualization should not be dismissed by linking it to the stifling rigidities of habituated behavior.

For the purposes of this argument, habituation can be referred to as the practice of such rites as baptism in a way that the tradition denies the culture(s) of those involved in the rite. It can therefore be suggested that such a rite would be mundane and removed of all drama, seen by those performing it just as something that ought to be done. In this sense the 'ought to be done' can be seen as tradition imposing itself on culture without being mindful of culture's own categories, dynamics and intrinsic laws.

Hence habituation is the bane of ritualization, it 'denies' the social drama of coming together and pushing apart, the actions that should be performed culturally by means of a tradition that is ritual and not habit. This supposes that rites are not givens, they have been referred to 'hand-me-down quilts' that are continually patched; they change, they are not rigid structures—or at least they ought to be.

To better understand 'what ought to be going on' in terms of ritualization, it is important not to repeat the series of explanations of the concept that were provided in the previous chapter. Thus sparing redundancy. However in light of that which has been described and discussed above, as well as understanding 'what ought to be going on', it is necessary to make use of certain explanations that have been drawn on in the previous chapter. Firstly, ritualization has been described as intentionally developing or inventing rituals on the margins of existing rituals. Secondly ritualization can be explained as that which leads to the formation of rituals. Thirdly, it is critical to the function of ritualization that it be noted that ritualization drives humans in culturally specific ways. Lastly ritualization, in terms of ethology, can be explained as formalized activities. The relevance of re-mentioning these explanations was in the aim of developing a working definition. The reason behind developing a working definition is to aid in understanding 'what ought to be going on' within the context of the research problem. By considering the working definition as ritualization norm, understanding what ought to be going on as well as learning from good practise can be achieved. The following, for the purposes of this normative inquiry, is a working definition of ritualization:

Ritualization leads to the formation of rituals. Rituals begin with ritualization, which can be described as formalized activities. Ritualization is not only the invention of rituals, it is also the development or renewal of already established rituals—driven in culturally specific ways.

This presupposes that if the baptismal rite, noted in the participant observation, has been or is continually ritualized it would not be a habituated event. The reason for ritualization of such rites is culture. As the liturgy is inculturated so the quilt, that is the ritual, has patches added to it. Like the 'patches' are added to the 'quilt' so are cultures connected to rituals through ritualization. In terms of 'what ought to be going on', if the ritual has been ritualized then the worshippers, for example, can enact, perform and engage in the ritual processes. If there is enactment, performance and engagement there is the presupposition of meaning and not the imposing of a mundane, habituated, 'ought to be' event.

The subsection below, which is the conclusion to this liturgical-ritual section, draws on the discussions above. By doing so the normative similarities of the functions of liturgical inculturation and ritualization will be described. The aim of these descriptions is to better understand the research problem, which is: how does the form and content of prayer impact the ways in which people connect with God and other people? This is asked from a normative perspective, by understanding what ought to be going on.

4.2.3. Liturgical-inculturation, Ritualization and Good Practice

Scrutiny can be placed on the research problem in order to better understand the role this section has in understanding the research problem. Ritualization and liturgical inculturation are concerned with form and content. In terms of this study both functions are of concern in understanding the impact of form and content, by means of learning from good practise.

Philosophically speaking it could be argued that the worship service can only be deemed as such if the worshippers validate it as such. In other words, if the worshippers are connected to God and each other through worship—which defines the community, reminding it both of its identity and its destiny—then what is going on is what ought to be going on. Christian worship is at the heart of Christian life where believers encounter

God's presence as individuals and as a collective. This refers again to the concept of *koinonia*, the fellowship between worshipper and God as well as the fellowship between worshippers. In prayer, whether ritualized or extemporaneous, worshippers gesture towards God and one another which is where connectedness ought to occur. Liturgical inculturation and ritualization are concerned with both aspects of said connectedness. As a result both concepts focus on the relationships between tradition (anthropological context) and culture, furthermore both are of the understanding that their processes are continuous, or ongoing.

From the perspectives of both liturgical inculturation and ritualization, tradition should not be imposed on or deny culture. Liturgical inculturation and ritualization are therefore bilateral notions. In other words tradition should not only affect culture, nor should culture only affect tradition. The former would be an imposition, the latter would be a type of consumerism—that which protects the interests of culture only. When considering ritualization, or ritualizing, from a liturgical perspective the cultural aspects that influence inculturation can be seen by using different approaches. These approaches include ritualizing through: the interaction of different meaning systems, the restoration of the unity of the domains of modern art and liturgy, recontextualization and shaping the liturgical ritual through bricolage. In terms of this study, as described in the above, referring to culture is not only referring to one's heritage but a matrix of aspects. All of the approaches listed above are inherently culturally driven, each considers a component that is culturally relevant.

The aim of any of the approaches mentioned above is the renewal of tradition, that which creates a new entity. One that includes cultures and that which is relevant to worshippers, thus worshippers can identify elements of their own cultures in experiencing and performing liturgical rituals. The reverse is also a possibility, by the insertion of tradition into culture, or certain cultural aspects, liturgical rituals—so to speak—are still renewed, thus they are culturally relevant. By means of experiencing an inculturated, or ritualized, liturgical ritual there is inclusivity and unity. Through culture 'accepting' tradition and vice versa worshippers are then included in what is going on. This is resonated by worshippers being able to identify certain cultural elements that are relevant to them, therefore including them in the liturgical ritual which they can experience and perform in unity with other worshippers. It should be mentioned that when referring to rituals, and/or liturgical rituals, what is essentially being referred to is prayer. Therefore it can be argued that if prayer is inculturated or ritualized in terms of the above, then its form and content impact the way in which people—or worshippers—connect with God and other people—or worshippers.

The completion of this chapter, in addition to the previous chapter, brings to the end the interpretive aspects. Insight has been gained by interpreting certain episodes, situations and contexts by drawing on theological concepts from the fields of Ecclesiology and Liturgical Studies as well as those from Ritual Studies. As a result of these interpretations better understandings and clearer insights have been gained into: *koinonia* and the creative tensions between unity and diversity, identity and otherness as well as inclusivity and exclusivity; the interrelationships between prayer, belief and living together/being church; as well as further development of the integrative aspects of liturgical inculturation and ritualization. The result is learning 'good practice' from this gained insights and the better understanding of the core concepts. By taking into great consideration that which has been gained by these two chapters, the fourth and final question can be asked in the following chapter: 'How might we respond?'

Chapter 5

A Sense of Belonging

Throughout the processes of the previous two chapters, the interpretations relayed back to the working hypothesis and the development thereof. By gaining further insights through interpretation, it was better understood how the importantly ongoing process of liturgical inculturation could aid the impact that the form and content of prayer have on people connecting with God and other people in the worship service. This chapter aims at responding to all that has been described and interpreted with a twofold suggested theory for praxis, by means of integrating all the insights. The final task, suggested by Osmer, includes determining plans for action that influence situations in ways that are desirable as well as entering into a reflective discussion. Therefore this chapter serves as a response not only to the empirical descriptions and interpretations but also the research problem, which is 'how does the form and content of prayer impact the ways in which people connect with God and other people?'. By conducting the relevant research and interpreting it through various arts and sciences insight has been gained into how the form and content of prayers impact the ways in which people connect with God and other people. Thus enabling the opportunity to respond in the form of a theory for praxis.

When suggesting a theory for praxis, aspects of which may be new to the field, it is important to remember that the aim is not to invent something brand new but rather adjust and re-invent what is already in practise. Life is not possible if the manner in which people act and engage with each other and God is completely re-invented anew constantly. From the perspectives of Liturgical Studies and Ritual Studies there is much concern placed on ongoing or continuous development and re-inventing, as well as the critical-reciprocal interactions advocated by liturgical inculturation. To clarify any contradictions that may be noticed in the above, from the perspectives mentioned above the process of re-inventing is one that maintains traditions by including cultures, which is congruent with the notion of liturgical inculturation. What is meant by this is that re-invention appropriates a tradition to a culture, thereby making the tradition relevant to the culture(s) performing and/or participating the aspects of the tradition.

As described in the introductory chapter, the Republic of South Africa epitomises cultural diversity. Within the worship service this diversity creates a tension with unity, from an ecclesiological perspective. The relationships between unity and diversity as well as that of inclusivity and exclusivity were discussed in the previous chapter. The section below addresses the South African context with special regard to the South African urban context.

5.1. THE SOUTH AFRICAN URBAN CONTEXT AND THE IMPORTANCE OF UNITY, INCLUSIVITY AND LITURGICAL INCULTURATION

The section title above includes three concepts which for the purposes of this research project, and all that has been interpreted, are similar in their notions. Whether unity or inclusivity as ecclesiological notions or inculturation as a liturgical notion, each of them presupposes, among other aspects, the same idea—inclusion, exclusion and the tension between them. In a multicultural setting such as the City of Centurion there are two factors that warrant the focus on unity, inclusivity and inculturation: firstly, the cultural diversity within the city and secondly, the post-apartheid context of South Africa. This is to consider liturgy, and its role in inclusivity, as an expression of all the people of God, whereby all such people 'need' to have their voices heard—a liturgy that is enacted without the distinctions of 'otherness'. Such a need to have one and all voices heard, in all spheres of life, is a current trend in South Africa especially with regard to the rights of individuals and groups, the inclusivity and equality of races and class, and the embracing of cultures and their various expressions. However, such needs—in an uncontrolled environment, whether liturgically or politically—can have a negative, somewhat anarchistic effect. As such, Volf explains that one's culture should be secondary to one's declarations of faith, also illustrating that: "At the very core of Christian identity lies an all-encompassing change of loyalty, from a given culture with its gods to the God of all cultures."[1] A similar notion is proposed by the Lutheran World Federation's Nairobi Statement that worship, among other aspects, be of counter-cultural nature, which entails the contextualization of Christian faith and worship thereby "challenging of all types of oppression and social injustice wherever they exist in earthly cultures" as well as transforming cultural patterns that: "idolise the self or the local group at the expense of a wider humanity."[2]

Muchimba writes: "I am strongly convinced that if an indigenous group had only a Bible, they would practice their worship in a manner that would be relevant to their culture and within a biblical framework."[3] The idea, shared by Muchimba, illustrates the presupposition that without the dictations of tradition, cultures would worship in their own biblically appropriate ways. This is, however, a romantic ideal which is used purely to illustrate how people contextualize and/or appropriate worship and worshipping through their cultures. Within an urban area however, the above idea raises a question: how does a multicultural church enable its attendees to worship in a manner that is relevant to their cultures? The answer, as a result of there being withstanding traditions, involves liturgical inculturation and liturgical interculturation. In support of the claim that there are withstanding traditions because Western culture was (and often still is) carried into a local culture along with the Christian message. As a result, this comes at a cost to the local culture and the message of the Gospel.

The aphoristic concept of *lex orandi, lex credendi, lex (con)vivendi* when translated refers to 'we' as in: 'as we pray'. Presupposing that the 'we' should be the entire, inclusive community of worshippers, then the ideal would be that all are involved in praying, believing and living together. This ideal can be assisted by liturgical inculturation, resulting in unity and inclusivity. As cultures are not static, liturgical inculturation should be an ongoing process to maintain the 'we' element in the notion of *lex orandi, lex credendi, lex (con)vivendi*. From the information gathered from the interviews conducted at all three churches involved in the research process, it could be deduced that the level of satisfaction with the worship service conveyed by the interviewees, in answering the seventh question asked in

---

1. Volf, *Exclusion and Embrace*, 40.
2. Lutheran World Federation. *Nairobi statement*, 4.
3. Muchimba, *Liberating the African soul*, 6.

the semi-structured interviews—can be associated with the process of liturgical inculturation. The responses to the aforementioned question from the semi-structured interviews could aid liturgical inculturation by means of revealing the 'wants' (culture) of the worshippers, of which tradition could embrace and/or critically reject. Thus this suggested theory for praxis continues the ongoing process of liturgical inculturation, maintaining that A (liturgy) + B (culture) = C (a new entity/liturgical inculturation).

As mentioned above, the continual process of liturgical inculturation is imperative to unity and inclusivity in the multicultural, post-apartheid context of South Africa. Inclusivity suggests, as mentioned in the previous chapter, the Pauline notion of the body of Christ. In terms of multicultural diversity, exclusivity suggests members of the church (attendees) as members of an association such as that of a golf club while inclusivity, or the body of Christ, suggests membership that is more akin to being a 'limb' or 'membrane' of Christ's body. In other words, an inseparable part of the worshipping community. It is within these metaphors that a realisation takes place, namely that the responsibility of liturgical inculturation, unity and inclusivity does not fall solely on church authorities but on all that are participating, attending and interacting in the worship service. This realisation can also be referred to as an epiphany, one that aids the understanding of the inseparable interrelations in the worship service—where a conversation has begun which cannot, ever, end. This is furthered by comprehending that mutual relationships are practiced with one's entire being, from the physical body itself to the emotions and the mind, from what is experienced through sight and hearing to what is said and done. How Christian people perform in worship, their actions through taking communion, their communication with others, and care for the needy are all bodily practices and not abstract concepts of community and Pastoral Care.

The idea conveyed above is similar to that which participatory action research aims to achieve through its proponents. In this case, the worshippers are the 'change agents'. This idea is a utopian ideal, similarly to that of the 'invisible' church which focusses on church unity—that the church is already one, that all believers share a mutual belief in God. Therefore this ideal is not immediately achievable in the 'here' and 'now', which is why liturgical inculturation cannot happen as an isolated incident but should be ongoing day by day, month by month, year by year, with the goal being that the 'invisible' church of what ought to be going on could be appropriated to that which is going on. Therefore the suggested theory for praxis begins with the idea that liturgical inculturation should be a continuous process with the aims not only of developing a new entity, an inculturated and interculturated liturgy, but that such an entity would serve the worshippers in the forms of unity and inclusivity in the worship service. In other words, that all worshippers would be inclusive and included in the body of Christ, in the fellowship of believers who have a joint share—through common participation—in the body of Christ.

The importance of liturgical inculturation, unity and inclusivity when considering the South African contexts of multicultural settings and post-apartheid democracy, is that through these concepts the exclusive member, the 'I', of the worship service can be transformed to the inclusive member, 'we'—living together in fellowship with other members of the body of Christ. Therefore, in the South African context, liturgical interculturation and inculturation proposed with the notions of unity and inclusivity can serve the worship service by maintaining the 'we' status of *lex orandi, lex credendi, lex (con)vivendi*. In other words: as 'we' pray and worship as a result of an inculturated liturgy, so should 'we' believe, think and talk, so should 'we' live, converse and relate with each and everyone—together. The reverse—*lex (con)vivendi, lex credendi, lex orandi*—could serve as the motivation behind liturgical inculturation in the South African contexts mentioned above. In other words by living together in attempted unity and inclusivity, so should 'we' believe in this unity and inclusivity, therefore so should 'we' pray in unity and inclusivity.

A conclusion can be drawn that liturgical inculturation in the South African context aids unity and inclusivity in the worship service as well as in the local and faith communities, from the perspective of *lex orandi, lex credendi, lex (con)vivendi*. Within the South African context, the importance of unity and inclusivity stretches beyond the faith communities into a nationwide objective as the population moves forward, ideally together—inclusively, from the history of the previous apartheid regime and the exclusivity of 'the other' that was caused along with loathing, distrust and paranoia among people. The conclusive statement above leads to required explanations on how this should be practiced. Therefore the section below, and its subsections, detail a suggested theory for praxis as a pragmatic response to the various interpretations of empirical data in the previous chapters.

5.2. CONNECTING WITH GOD AND OTHER PEOPLE THROUGH PRAYER

As a result of the intended aim of this suggested theory having dual outcomes, namely (1) connectedness with God and (2) connectedness with other people through prayer, this suggested theory for praxis is twofold. Liturgical inculturation as an ongoing process, as described above, plays a large role in the suggested theory for praxis. As a result this section has been divided into two subsections. Each of which explain the suggested theory for praxis in terms of one of the outcomes above. It is intended that the two outcome based aspects are practiced simultaneously due to the understanding that in 'the body of Christ' concept of fellowship sees said body bound together in corporate solidarity where Christ "joins the vertical and horizontal dimensions of our life together, uniting us through the Spirit with God and one another".[4] Long illustrates this notion by writing that: " . . . we human beings hunger for both God and community, or to put it more precisely, we hunger for God in community".[5] In other words, the suggested theory for praxis consists of two components that function interdependently as one. The first component, discussed below, is exclusive connectedness which is described as the connection between the worshipper as an individual and God.

5.2.1. Exclusive Connectedness and a Sense of Belonging

In the introduction it was mentioned that people have different perceptions, or beliefs of God that are illustrated by what they believe and how they pray. Within the inclusive-exclusive tension of being church, such 'mystical perceptions' are personal and therefore exclusive, as the significance of this perception is that it constitutes a fundamentally important part of the personal relationship with God. With the understanding that human beings hunger for both God and community, this subsection focusses on the exclusive, vertical elements of communion, or connectedness, with God. Whilst congregations are inherently spaces where community cannot be escaped. In prayer one can privately experience God's 'mystical' presence whilst praying simultaneously with others thus activating one's personal relationship with God through their exclusive mystical perceptions or

4. Van Deusen Hunsinger, *Practicing Koinonia*, 347.
5. Long, *Beyond the worship wars*, 30.

beliefs. This is to suggest that in the worship service a worshipper, whilst praying simultaneously with others, can express their personal, exclusive needs. Therefore connecting exclusively with God in prayer through the same form but personalized content.

The above suggests that, using the body of Christ concept, the 'right arm' whilst part of the body can function independently to the 'left arm'. A metaphorical explanation can be provided to aid the understanding of this notion: whilst the whole body is driving a vehicle, similarly to the entire congregation praying simultaneously, the one arm is operating the steering wheel whilst the other arm is alternating gears by using the gear lever. It is possible in accordance with this explanation that one worshipper, albeit the one arm or the other, can pray in simultaneous form as all others, such as the whole body being in the act of driving, yet pray different content to all others. What can be concluded is that people (worshippers) have many different experiences within worship, and of worship, and therefore many different impressions of worship and prayer.

In congruence with the above the suggested theory for praxis, which is intended as a continuation of liturgical inculturation, should aid exclusive connectedness that maintains a sense of belonging. This should fulfil one of the two profound human needs: the need for communion with God. It should be remembered that this notion functions interdependently and simultaneously with the second notion, which fulfils the second of the profound human needs.

It has been explained in previous chapters that when referring to culture, what is being referred to is a complex matrix of factors that result in the uniqueness, exclusiveness, of a person. Therefore, this subsection and the notion of exclusive connectedness suggests a theory for praxis by adapting the process of liturgical inculturation to focus on said exclusiveness and one's personal relationship with God in the worship service. The research problem asks how the form and content of prayer impact the ways in which people connect with God and other people. This subsection focusses on exclusive connectedness with God.

When considering the process of liturgical inculturation, a series of questions should be asked of tradition and culture. Such questions are imperative to the notion of exclusive connectedness and can be adapted for the purpose of said connectedness. Therefore, as part of this ongoing process of liturgical inculturation, the following question can be asked: to what extent is this prayer form a relevant expression regarding the content that impacts experiences of exclusive spirituality of the celebrating persons? Another suggested question that should be asked with an eye on liturgy in the making is: To what extent is this liturgy reflecting the contextual realities of where it is celebrated? Like the questions above, this question focusses on the worshippers and their experiences which are both exclusive and inclusive.

These questions are both examples and suggestions, they are guidelines or ideas that can be used as is, adapted and/or added to. Providing a list of questions is not of immediate importance due to the fact that the focus of this suggested theory for praxis is the exclusive connectedness which can only be appropriated by the participants and their realities. Therefore such questions aimed at the role of culture can be developed when continuing the process of liturgical inculturation by a means of focussing on the exclusive connectedness of a worshipper, otherwise referred to as communion with God as a profound human need. The same notion is suggested for asking questions regarding the role of tradition. An example of such questions regarding the role of tradition is: to which voices from the past do you listen to and which ones do you ignore?

With regard to adaptions that can be made in the process of liturgical inculturation, the following is relevant to both the exclusive connectedness, discussed above, and the inclusive connectedness which will be discussed in the subsection below: "Sunday should become an experience of faith, a day of encounter between the community of the faithful and the risen Lord present in word and sacrament. But experience and encounter are cultural categories. They take place in the setting of a people's culture and are deeply influenced by it. If Sunday is to become part of a people's life, it must be grafted on their culture."[6] Without excluding tradition and the questions that should be asked of its role in liturgical inculturation, the grafting of tradition onto culture further suggests that questions should continually be developed. Such questions aimed at the role of culture should be developed in order to understand people's appropriations of experience and encounter of connectedness. These appropriations can allude to exclusive or inclusive connectedness—or both.

The above concludes the first of the two notions for the suggested theory for praxis. As described in the previous chapter, there is a tension created between exclusivity and inclusivity with regard to koinonia. This tension should not be ignored, hence there is a twofold approach to this

---

6. Chupungco, *Liturgies for the Future*, 184–85.

suggested theory for praxis. It was discussed in the previous chapter that, in ecclesiological terms, liturgical in(ter)culturation seeks to aid the exclusive in becoming inclusive. This was suggested as a result of the interpretation that one's exclusivity cannot be avoided although their inclusivity, or faith, in the worship service should be paramount. The section below discusses the second of the two notions for the suggested theory for praxis, which considers transforming the exclusive member to the inclusive member of the faith community.

5.2.2. Inclusive Connectedness and a Sense of Belonging

It has been established that there are two profound human needs that worship, and prayer, should meet. The first need, communion with God, has been discussed above. There are two concepts that will be discussed below with regard to inclusivity and unity in the faith community: (1) the need for human community and (2) the desire for God in community.

When the interviewees were asked "Do you engage in prayer? If so, how often?" The question was most often met with responses that suggested multiple prayers on a daily basis. Such is the notion of *lex orandi, lex credendi, lex vivendi* that worshippers live their beliefs in their day-to-day lives and not just on Sundays in the worship service. In the previous chapter the concept of a septuple rhythm was mentioned and, whether in terms of exclusive or inclusive connectedness, the worship service and the prayers within it should be relative to the day-to-day experiences of the worshipper. The intention of suggesting this goes further than contextual experiences such as praying for rain during a nationwide drought, it suggests that experiences and encounters of connectedness impacted through the form and content of prayer, in the worship service should compliment the connectedness experienced and/or encountered in the day-to-day prayers of the worshippers. Under the informed assumption, as a result of the interview data, that one experiences and/or encounters connectedness in their "quiet time" and other personal daily prayer rituals, similar experiences should be available in the worship service. This is achievable and measurable through appropriation, whether the worship service is seen as a conclusive response to the week before it or if the week is an extension of the worship service which begins it.

Inclusive connectedness denotes unity and inclusivity in the worship service. In other words it appropriates the worshippers' sense of belonging to the faith community and that community's sense of belonging to God. This sense of belonging hinges on the relevance of the worship service to the culture(s) of the worshippers. When considering the questions that could be asked of the roles of culture and tradition what can be noticed is that the questions pertain to the relevance of tradition and/or culture. The relevance of either in terms of the other is where the critical-reciprocal interaction between tradition and culture begins—and should continue. This critical-reciprocal interaction extends through all the relevant elements of the worship service and being church, such as the prayers from the worship manuals as well as extemporaneous prayers. The proposed outcome of liturgical inculturation is the adaptation of the worship service, a new entity developed by the continuous critical-reciprocal interactions between tradition and culture.

Adaptation can be described as the process whereby the worship service and all its connected elements and practices are given alternative forms that correspond with the cultures and traditions of the church. Therefore, in the process of liturgical inculturation, tradition (liturgy) criticizes and/or rejects some aspects of culture and embraces others, and vice versa. A suggested theory for praxis with regard to liturgical inculturation is that questions should be developed that focus on the roles of tradition and culture in aiding unity and inclusivity in the worship service. The focus on unity and inclusivity, within the process of liturgical inculturation, should then aid how the form and content of prayer impacts the ways in which people connect with God and other people. Therefore, the continual development of understanding the relevance of tradition and culture to the worshippers will, through the adaptation of the form and content of prayer, impact communion with God and communion with other people. This should lead to the worshippers' profound human need being met by experiencing God in community, which can be described as actualising the Pauline notion of the body of Christ. Congregations are, at the end of the day, groups of people that have a fundamental institutional structure and have gathered together with a purpose. Congregational worship is not the same as private worship because it creates an awareness of others, as well as their social, ethical and moral expectations and demands.

In aiding unity and inclusivity, the process of liturgical inculturation can make use of such aspects as ritualization. If awareness of the other discloses social and ethical expectation and demands, it can be speculated that worshippers expect inclusivity through invitation, mutual understanding and relevant, or common, participation in liturgical rituals for example. The adverse can then also be ethically expected, for example one is expected to invite the other into the 'circle'. Here again is a space for conversations to be had and questions to be asked with regard to the relevant roles of tradition and culture. Proverbially speaking, these conversations allow for tradition to better understand culture and vice versa. Worshippers "depend heavily on psychosomatically informed processes like 'being moved', 'feeling the spirit' or 'having a full heart'. Such conversations of liturgical inculturation should aid the appropriation of these processes by renewing, or adapting, traditions in accordance with the cultural relevance of the worshippers. The notion of ritualization drives people in culturally specific ways, Tom Long suggests that: "If we listen carefully, we can hear this hunger for God in community in the cries of our culture."[7]

With regard to the suggested theory for praxis, the process of liturgical inculturation goes beyond listening carefully to the cries of culture by listening as attentively to tradition. Thus conducting the ongoing critical-reciprocal interactions between tradition and culture. If worshippers—driven by culturally specific ways—are crying out to 'be moved', said worshippers are crying out for tradition to be inclusive of their culture(s). Through liturgical inculturation and critical-reciprocal interactions, tradition is obliged to respond to these cries appropriately. As a result the relevant adaptations can be made—if necessary. Thus providing alternative liturgical and/or ritual forms that correspond relevantly with culture and tradition.

This concludes the twofold suggested theory for praxis. The intention of the above is to contribute to what should be an ongoing process, namely liturgical inculturation. That which is suggested is the additional focus on inclusivity and unity that aid 'being church'. Below are some final remarks that conclude the pragmatic response that has been assisted by asking: 'What is going on?', 'Why is this going on?' and 'what ought to be going on?'

5.3. CONCLUDING THE PRAGMATIC RESPONSE

Throughout this chapter the term 'relevance' has been mentioned on numerous occasions when describing and discussing the importance of liturgical inculturation in the (urban) South African contexts that are both multicultural and in lieu of living in the post-apartheid era. It should be

7. Long, *Beyond the worship wars*, 30.

remembered that Senn suggests that: "every generation of Christians has been concerned that its worship be relevant, at least to them."[8] The processes of liturgical interculturation and liturgical inculturation are imperative in aiding this relevance in a multicultural context. Beyond the multicultural context, unity and inclusivity aid relevance in being church in post-apartheid South Africa. Also within this multicultural context, relevance can be counter-cultural as the identity of the 'I' may become inclusive with 'the other' in 'other spaces', which is potentially heterotopia.

According to binary thinking, inclusivity and exclusivity has provided a challenge since the apostles' early proclamation of the Gospel. Therefore there is a history of a creative tension between inclusivity and exclusivity, as a result of the diversity of humanity and the challenge of dealing with otherness. 'What ought to be going on' is a creative tension between inclusivity (unity) and exclusivity (diversity). This creative tension can be maintained by liturgical inculturation, by means of ongoing critical-reciprocal interactions between cult (liturgy) and culture that criticise, reject and embrace one another. Thus this suggested theory for praxis is a contribution to the liturgia condenda, or liturgy in the making—liturgy for the future.

As the suggested theory for praxis liturgical inculturation should, through critical-reciprocal interactions aid the relevance of the worshippers that worship and pray (*lex orandi*) in corresponds with tradition and their beliefs (*lex credendi*). This should then aid the worshippers' unity and inclusivity in 'being church', in living together—with one another (*lex (con) vivendi*). Therefore, liturgical inculturation with a focus on unity and inclusivity should affect praying, believing and being church.

The process of liturgical inculturation, as a concept, is an ongoing one. This concept can be developed by further studies and empirical research. By further developing the concept or making a contribution thereto, the practice of liturgical inculturation can be developed to more effectively aid its function. Therefore it can be suggested that further research can be conducted not only on the liturgy as a whole but as a series of ritual acts. By focussing on particular acts or elements of the liturgy, rather than the liturgy as a whole, smaller new entities are created. Such smaller new entities could, for example, be as a result of ritualization. Each of these smaller new entities culminate in creating a larger new entity—an inculturated liturgy. Another possible method for further developing the field of liturgical inculturation, through studies and/or empirical research, is to consider

---

8. Senn, *Christian Worship*, 38.

the concept from the perspectives of different fields or by combining disciplines. In considering liturgical inculturation, liturgists have drawn from the fields of Ritual Studies, anthropology and sociology—for example. It could be beneficial to consider perspectives from the field of musicology for example—incorporating the form and function of sounds and music, harmonies and melodies, crescendos and diminuendos. Furthermore, it has become increasingly important to consider, examine, research and/or develop, what has been referred to as, liturgical inculturation from the lived experience and/or from the perspective of lived religion.

Bibliography

Ackermann, Denise M. "Becoming Fully Human: an Ethic of Relationship in Difference and Otherness." *Journal of Theology of Southern Africa* 102 (1998) 13–27.
Allen, Pauline, et al. *Prayer and Spirituality in the Early Church, Volume 1.* Centre for Early Christian Studies. Queensland: Australian Catholic University, 1998.
Allen, Pauline, et al., *Prayer and Spirituality in the Early Church, Volume 2.* Centre for Early Christian Studies. Queensland: Australian Catholic University, 1999.
Ammerman, Nancy T. *Studying Congregations : a New Handbook.* Nashville: Abingdon, 1998.
Babbie, Earl and Mouton, Johan. *The Practice of Social Research.* Cape Town: Oxford University Press, 2001.
Baker, Joseph O. "An Investigation of the Sociological Patterns of Prayer Frequency and Content." *Sociology of religion* 69(2) (2008) 169–85.
Bänziger, Sarah, et al. "Praying in a Secularised Society: an Empirical Study of Praying Practices and Varieties." *The International Journal for the Psychology of Religion* 18(3) (2008) 256–65.
Barnard, Marcel. "Flows of worship in the network society: Liminality as heuristic concept in Practical Theology beyond action theory." *In die Skriflig* 44(1) (2010) 67–84.
Barnard, Marcel, et al. *Worship in the Network Culture: Liturgical Ritual Studies: Fields and Methods, Concepts and Metaphors.* Liturgia condenda, 28. Leuven: Peeters, 2014.
Bell, Catherine. *Ritual: Perspectives and Dimensions.* New York: Oxford University Press, 1997.
Bosman, Lourens and Müller, Julian. "'n Narratiewe benadering tot die Liturgie." *Verbum et Ecclesia* 30(2) (2009) 6 pages.
Bouteneff, Peter C. "Koinonia and Eucharistic Unity." *Liturgy* 20(4) (2005) 57–65.
———. "Ecumenical Ecclesiology and the Language of Unity." *Journal of Ecumenical Studies* 44(3) (2009), 352–60.
Browning, Don S. *A Fundamental Practical Theology.* Minneapolis: Augsburg Fortress, 1991.
Brown, Frank B. *Inclusive Yet Discerning: Navigating Worship Artfully.* Grand Rapids: Eerdmans (The Calvin Institute of Christian Worship Liturgical Studies series), 2009.
Brown, Laurence B. *The Human Side of Prayer: the Psychology of Praying.* Birmingham, Alaska: Religious Education Press, 1994.
Brümmer, Vincent. *What are We Doing When we Pray? A Philosophical Inquiry.* London: SCM, 1984.

Bibliography

———, "Spirituality and the hermeneutics of faith." *HTS Theological Studies* 66(1) (2010) 5 pages.

Bryant, Antony & Charmaz, Kathy. eds. *The SAGE Handbook of Grounded Theory*. London: SAGE Publications Ltd, 2007.

Carter, David, "Ecumenical Ecclesiology: Unity, Diversity and Otherness in a Fragmented World." *Ecclesiology* 7(3) (2011) 403–6.

Charmaz, Kathy. *Constructing Grounded Theory: A Practical Guide through Qualitative Analysis*. Thousand Oaks: SAGE Publications, 2006.

Chupungco, Anscar J. *Liturgies for the Future*. Eugene, OR: Wipf and Stock, 1982.

———. *Cultural Adaptation of the Liturgy*. Eugene, OR: Wipf and Stock, 1982.

———. *Liturgical Inculturation: Sacramentals, Religiosity, and Catechesis*. Collegeville: The Liturgical Press, 1992.

Coghlan, David and Brydon-Miller, Mary. *The Sage Encyclopedia of Action Research, Volume 2*. London: SAGE Publications Ltd, 2014.

Crawford, Janet and Best, Thomas F. "Praise the Lord with the Lyre... and the Gamelan?: Towards Koinonia in Worship." *The Ecumenical Review* 46(1) (1994) 78–96.

Cullman, Oscar. *Prayer in the New Testament*. London: SCM, 1995.

Davison, Scott A. "Petitionary Prayer." *The Stanford Encyclopedia of Philosophy (Summer 2017 Edition)*, Edward N. Zalta (ed.), https://plato.stanford.edu/archives/sum2017/entries/petitionary-prayer/.

Denny, Lindy and Wepener, Cas J., "The Spirit and the Meal As a Model for Charismatic Worship: A Practical-Theological Exploration: Original Research." *HTS : Theological Studies* 69(1) (2013) 1–9.

De Klerk, B. J. "Liturgiese Identiteitsvorming As Antwoord Op Die Invloed Van Die Verbruikerskultuur." *In die Skriflig/In Luce Verbi* 34(4) (2000) 451–68.

De Vos, A. S., et al. *Research at grass roots, 4th Edition*. Pretoria: Van Schaik, 2011.

Ekman, Paul, "Facial expression and emotion." *American psychologist* 48(4) (1993) 384.

———. *Emotions revealed: Recognizing faces and feelings to improve communication and emotional life*. Macmillan, 2003.

Finney, John R. and Newton Maloney, H. Jr. "Empirical studies of Christian prayer: a review of the literature." *Journal of Psychology & Theology* 13(2) (1985) 104–15.

Foucault, Michel & Miskowiec, Jay. "Of other spaces." *Diacritics* 16(1) (1986) 22–27.

Fuist, Todd N. "Talking to God among a Cloud of Witnesses: Collective Prayer As a Meaningful Performance." *Journal for the Scientific Study of Religion* 54(3) (2015) 523–39.

Gräb, Wilhelm. "Practical Theology as theology of religion: Schleiermacher's understanding of Practical Theology as a discipline." *International Journal Of Practical Theology* 9(2) (2005) 181–96.

Geertz, Clifford. *The interpretation of cultures*. New York: Basic Books, 1973.

Gerkin, Charles. *An introduction to Pastoral Care*. Nashville: Abingdon, 1997.

Gilbert, Kathleen. *The Emotional Nature of Qualitative Research*. Boca Raton: CRC, 2001.

Given, Lisa M. *The sage encyclopedia of qualitative research methods*. Thousand Oaks, CA: SAGE Publications, Inc., 2008.

Grimes, Ronald L. *Beginnings in Ritual Studies*, Third Edition. Waterloo, Canada: Ritual Studies International, 2010.

———. *Deeply into the Bone: Re-inventing Rites of Passage*. University of California Press, 2000.

Bibliography

———. *Ritual, media, and conflict* (ORS; Oxford Ritual Studies).New York: Oxford University Press, 2011.

Gubrium, Jaber F., et al. *The SAGE handbook of interview research: The complexity of the craft*. Thousand Oaks, CA: SAGE Publications Ltd, 2012.

Heitink, Gerben. *Practical Theology: history, theory, action domains*. Translated by Bruinsma, R., Grand Rapids, OR: Eerdmans, 1999.

Hendriks, Jurgens. *Studying congregations in Africa*. Wellington, South Africa: Lux Verbi, 2004.

Herrera, Marina. "Popular Devotions and Liturgical Education." *Liturgy* 5(1) (2009) 33–37.

Hutchings, Paul B. and Sullivan, Katie E. "Prejudice and the Brexit vote: a tangled web." *Palgrave Commun* 5(5) (2019).

Immink, Gerrit F. "The Sense of God's Presence in Prayer." *HTS Teologiese Studies/ Theological Studies* 72(4) (2016).

James Baesler, E. and Chen, Yi-Fan. "Mapping the Landscape of Digital Petitionary Prayer as Spiritual/Social Support in Mobile,Facebook, and E-mail." *Journal of Media and Religion* 12(1) (2013).

Janssen, Jacques A. P. J., et al. "The Structure and Variety of Prayer." *Journal of Empirical Theology* 13 (2) (2000) 29–54.

Jenkins, Phillip. *The Next Christendom: The Coming of Global Christianity*. New York: Oxford University Press, 2011.

Kärkkäinen, Veli-Matti. *An Introduction to Ecclesiology: Ecumenical, Historical & Global Perspectives*. Downers Grove: Intervarsity Press, 2002.

Karris, Robert J. *Prayer and the New Testament*. New York: The Crossroad Publishing Company, 2000.

Keltner, Dacher, et al. 'Facial expression of emotion.' In *Handbook of Emotions, 2nd Edition*, edited by Michael Lewis et al. New York: Guilford Publications, 2003.

Klein, Julie T. and Newell, William H. *Advancing interdisciplinary studies*. In *Handbook of the Undergraduate Curriculum: A Comprehensive Guide to Purposes, Structures, Practices, and Change*, edited by Jerry G. Gaff and James L. Ratcliff, 393–415. San Francisco: Jossey-Bass, 1997.

Klein, Julie T. "The Rhetoric of Interdisciplinarity: Boundary Work in the Construction of New Knowledge.' In *The Sage Handbook of Rhetorical Studies*, edited by Andrea A. Lunsford et al. SAGE Publications, Inc, 2009.

Klomp, Mirella, et al., eds. *Rond de tafel: Maaltijd Vieren in Liturgische Contexten*. Heeswijk: Berne Media, 2018.

Klomp, Mirella. *The Sound of Worship: Liturgical Performance by Surinamese Lutherans and Ghanaian Methodists in Amsterdam*. Liturgia condenda, 26. Leuven: Peeters, 2011.

Krakowsky, Posey. "The Ecclesiology of Prayer Book Illustrations." *Anglican and Episcopal history* 83(3) (2014) 243–91.

Krause, Neal. "Assessing the Relationships among Prayer Expectancies, Race, and Self-Esteem in Late Life." *Journal for the Scientific Study of Religion* 43(3) (2004) 395–408.

Küng Hans. *The Church*. Tunbridge Wells, England: Burns & Oates, 1968.

Lathrop, Gordon. *Holy People: a Liturgical Ecclesiology*. Minneapolis: Fortress, 1999.

Littlejohn, Stephen W., and Foss, Karen A. *Theories of Human Communication: Tenth Edition*, Long Grove, IL: Waveland, 2011.

Bibliography

Long, Tom G. and Tisdale, Leanora T., eds. *Teaching Preaching as a Christian Practice: a New Approach to Homiletical Pedagogy*. Louisville: Westminster John Knox, 2008.

Long, Tom G. *Beyond the worship wars: building vital and faithful worship*. The Alban Institute, Inc, 2001.

Lukken, Gerard M. *Per Visibilia ad Invisibilia*. Leuven: Peeters, 1994.

———. "Liturgiewetenschappelijkonderzoek in Culturele Context. Metodischeverheldering en Vragen." *Jaarboek voor liturgie-onderzoek* 13 (1997) 135–48.

Lutheran World Federation. *Nairobi Statement on Worship and Culture: Contemporary Challenges and Opportunities*. Lutheran World Federation, Geneva, 1996.

———. "Chicago Statement on Worship and Culture: Baptism and Rites of Life Passage." *Studia Liturgica* 28 (1998) 244–52.

Mannion, Gerard and Mudge, Lewis S. eds. *The Routledge Companion to the Christian Church*. New York: Routledge (Routledge companion), 2010.

Mannion, Gerard. "Postmodern Ecclesiologies." In *The Routledge Companion to the Christian Church*, edited by Gerard Mannion and Lewis S. Mudge. New York: Routledge (Routledge companion), 2010.

Mbiti, John S. *African Religions and Philosophy*. London: Heinemann Educational Books, 1969.

McDougall, Joy A. "The Return of Trinitarian Praxis? Moltmann on the Trinity and the Christian life." *The Journal of Religion* 83(2) (2003) 177–203.

———. *Pilgrimage and Love: Moltmann on the Trinity and Christian life*. New York: Oxford University Press, 2005.

McGrath, Alister E. *Christian Theology: An Introduction*, Fourth Edition. Malden: Blackwell, 2007.

———. *Theology: the Basics*, Second Edition. Malden: Blackwell Publishing Ltd, 2004.

McKnight, Scot. "Ecclesiology." In *The Routledge Companion to Modern Christian Thought*, edited by Chad Meister and James Beilby. London: Routledge, 2013.

Methodist Conference Office. *The Methodist Service Book*. The Garden City Press Limited, 1975.

Miller-McLemore, Bonnie J. and Wiley-Blackwell (Firm). *The Wiley-Blackwell Companion to Practical Theology*. Malden: Wiley-Blackwell, 2014.

Moltmann, Jürgen. *The Trinity and the Kingdom: the Doctrine of God*, translated by Kohl, Margaret. London: SCM [1980] 1981.

———. *The Church in the Power of the Spirit: a Contribution to Messianic Ecclesiology*. Minneapolis: Fortress, 1993.

Muchimba, Felix. *Liberating the African Soul: Comparing African and Western Christian Music and Worship Styles*. Colorado Springs: Authentic Publishing, 2007

Mulder, Tim J. *So You've Been Asked to . . . Lead in Prayer*. Grand Rapids: Faith Alive Christian Resources, 1996.

Müller, Bethel A. and Wepener, Cas J. "Applying Grounded Theory to Data Collected Through Participatory Research on AIC Liturgical Rituals: A Comparative Study." *HTS Teologiese Studies/ Theological Studies* 67(2) (2011), 8 pages.

Old, Hughes O. *Leading in prayer: a workbook for ministers*. Grand Rapids: Eerdmans, 1995.

Osmer, Richard R. *Practical Theology: An Introduction*. Grand Rapids: Eerdmans, 2008.

O'Rourke, Michael, et al. "Introduction." In *Enhancing Communication & Collaboration in Interdisciplinary Research*. Thousand Oaks, CA: SAGE Publications, Inc. 1–10, 2014.

Pecklers, Keith F. *Worship*. Collegeville: The Liturgical Press, 2003.

Bibliography

Peterson, David. *Engaging with God: a Biblical Theology of Worship*, 1st North American Edition. Grand Rapids: Eerdmans, 1993.

Pieterse, H. J. C. *Preaching in the Context of Poverty*. Unisa Press, 2001.

———. "Grounded Theory Approach in Sermon Analysis of Sermons on Poverty and Directed at the Poor As Listeners." *Acta Theologica* 30(2) (2010) 113–29.

———. "A Grounded Theory Approach to the Analysis of Sermons on Poverty: Congregational Projects As Social Capital." *Verbum et Ecclesia* 33(1) (2010) 1–7.

Ponterotto, Joseph G. "Brief Note on the Origins, Evolution, and Meaning of the Qualitative Research Concept "Thick Description."" *The Qualitative Report* 11(3) (2003) 538–49.

Post, Paul. *Christian Feast and Festival: The Dynamics of Western Liturgy and Culture*. Liturgia condenda, 12. Leuven: Peeters, 2001.

———. *Ritual Studies*. Oxford Research Encyclopaedia of Religion, 2015.

———. *Voorbij het Kerkgebouw: De Speelruimte van Eenander Sacral Domein*. Heeswijk: Uitgeverij Abdij van Berne, 2010.

Ramshaw, Gail. *Liturgical Language: Keeping it Metaphorical, Making it Inclusive*. Collegeville: The Liturgical Press, 1996.

Rappaport, Roy A. *Ritual and Religion in the Making of Humanity*. Cambridge: University Press, 1999.

Reddie, Anthony G. *Black Theology, Slavery and Contemporary Christianity: 200 Years and No Apology*. Surrey, England: Ashgate, 2010.

———. "Do Black Lives Matter in Post-Brexit Britain?" *Studies in Christian Ethics*, 32(3) (2019) 387–401.

Repko, Allen F. and Szostak, Rick. *Interdisciplinary research: process and theory*, Fourth edition. Los Angeles: SAGE Publications, Inc., 2017.

Rossouw, Pieter F. "Inclusive Communities: A Missional Approach to Racial Inclusivity Within the Dutch Reformed Church." *Stellenbosch Theological Journal* 2(1) (2016) 381–96.

Schattauer, Thomas H. "Liturgical Studies: Disciplines, Perspectives, Teaching." *International Journal of Practical Theology* 11(1) (2007) 106–37.

Schuster, Marja. "Hermeneutics As Embodied Existence." *International Journal of Qualitative Methods* 12(1) (2013) 195–206.

Scott, Hilton R., Van Wyk, Tanya, & Wepener, Cas. "Prayer and Being Church in Postapartheid, Multicultural South Africa." *Verbum et Ecclesia* 40(1) (2019) a1964. https://doi.org/10.4102/ve.v40i1.1964

Scott, Hilton R. & Wepener, Cas J. "Healing as Transformation and Restoration: A Ritual-Liturgical Exploration." *HTS Theological Studies* 73(4) (2017), 9 pages. https://doi.org/10.4102/hts.v73i4.4064

———. "Ubuntu in the Worship Service as Heterotopia: A Liturgical-Ecclesiological Exploration." *In die Skriflig* 54(1) (2020) a2514. https://doi.org/10.4102/ids.v54i1.2514

Scott, Hilton R. "All Things Bright and Beautiful: Liturgy for Sustainable Living." *Stellenbosch Theological Journal | STJ* 7(1) (2021), 1–18. http://dx.doi.org/10.17570/stj.2021.v7n1.a07

———. "As We Live, So We Believe, So We Worship Together: a Liturgical Exploration into The Causal Interrelationships Between Lex Orandi, Lex Credendi, Lex (Con) Vivendi." *Stellenbosch Theological Journal | STJ* 7(2) (2021) 1–19. http://dx.doi.org/10.17570/stj.2021.v7n2.a5

Bibliography

———. "'Lest We Forget': a Postapartheid Perspective on Remembering in Liturgy for Healing and Justice." *Studia Liturgica* 51(1) (2021) 60–72. https://doi.org/10.1177/00393207209789 19

———. "Praying, Believing and Being Church A Ritual-Liturgical Exploration." *Yearbook for Ritual and Liturgical Studies* 34 (2018) summary of thesis. https://doi.org/10.21827/5bfeaae30dc20

———. "Worship in a Post-Lockdown Context: A Ritual-Liturgical Perspective." *HTS Teologiese Studies/Theological Studies* 76(1) (2020), a6112. https://doi.org/10.4102/hts.v76i1.6112

Senn, Frank C. *Christian Worship and its Cultural Setting*. Philadelphia: Fortress, 1983.

Smith, James K. A. *Desiring the Kingdom: Worship, Worldview, and Cultural Formation*. Grand Rapids, MI: Baker Academic, 2009.

Smith, Kevin G. "Review of Richard Osmer, Practical Theology: an introduction, R. R Osmer: book review." *Conspectus: The Journal of South African Theological Seminary* 10 (2010) 99–113.

Smit, Dirk J. "Lex orandi, lex credendi, lex (con)vivendi? - Oriënterende inleiding tot liturgie en etiek." *Nederduitse Gereformeerde Teologiese Tydskrif (NGTT)* 45(3-4) (2004) 887–907.

Spinks, Bryan D. "Anglicans and dissenters." in *The Oxford history of Christian Worship*, edited by Geoffrey Wainwright and Karen B. Westerfield Tucker. Oxford: Oxford University Press, 2006.

Statistics South Africa (StatsSA). *Census 2011 Census in brief*. 2011.

Stringer, Martin D. *On the perception of worship: the ethnography of worship in four Christian congregations in Manchester*. Birmingham: University of Birmingham Press, 1999.

Swinkels, T. and Post, Paul, "Beginnings in Ritual Studies according to Ronald Grimes." *Jaarboek voor Liturgie-onderzoek* 19 (2003) 215–38.

Szostak, Rick. "The interdisciplinary research process." In *Case studies in interdisciplinary research*, edited by Allen F. Repko et al., 3–20. Thousand Oaks, CA: SAGE Publications, Inc., 2012.

Tarasar, Constance J. "Worship, Spirituality and Biblical Reflection: Their Significance for the Churches' Search for Koinonia." *The Ecumenical Review* 45(2) (1993) 218–25.

Thiselton, Anthony C. *The hermeneutics of doctrine*. Grand Rapids: Eerdmans, 2007.

———. *Systematic Theology*. Grand Rapids: Eerdmans, 2015.

The Provincial Trustees of the Anglican Church of Southern Africa. *The Holy Eucharist from An Anglican Prayer Book*. 1989.

The Upper Room. Accessed from: http://devotional.upperroom.org [Accessed 13 April 2017].

Thumma, Scott L. "Methods for Congregational Study." In *Studying Congregations: a New Handbook*, edited by Nancy T. Ammerman et al. Nashville: Abingdon, 1998.

Turner, Victor R. *The Ritual Process: Structure and Anti-Structure*. London: Routledge & Kegan Paul, 1969.

———. *The Ritual Process: Structure and Anti-structure*. New York, NY: De Gruyter, 1995.

Van Buren, Abigail. "*Dear Abby... Sinners And Saints!*" Park City Daily News 5 (1964).

Van der Borght, Eddy. 'The Church As the Community of the Shared Story.' *Journal of Reformed Theology* 2(1) (2008) 5–16.

VandeCreek, Larry, et al. "Praying About Difficult Experiences As Self-Disclosure to God." *The International Journal for the Psychology of Religion* 12(1) (2002) 29–39.

Bibliography

Vanderwell, Howard. *Caring Worship: Helping Worship Leaders Provide Pastoral Care through the Liturgy*. Eugene, OR: Cascade Books, 2017.

Van Deusen Hunsinger, Deborah. "Practicing Koinōnia." *Theology Today* 66(3) (2009) 346–67.

Van Gennep, Arnold. *Les Rites de Passage*. Paris: Emile Nourry, 1909.

———. *The Rites of Passage*. London: Routledge & Kegan Paul, 1960.

van Ommen, Armand L. "Liturgy and Pastoral Care: Pastoral Worship and Priestly Counselling." *Studia Liturgica*, vol. 46(1–2) (2016) 208–21.

———. "Remembering for Healing: Liturgical Communities of Reconciliation Provide Space for Trauma." In *Trauma and Lived Religion: Transcending the Ordinary*, edited by Ruard Ganzevoort and Srdjan Sremac, 203–23. Palgrave Studies in Lived Religion and Societal Challenges, Palgrave Macmillan, 2019.

———. *Suffering in Worship: Anglican Liturgy in Relation to Stories of Suffering People*. Liturgy, Worship and Society Series. London: Routledge, 2017.

Van Wyk, Tanya. "Church as heterotopia: Original Research." *HTS: Theological Studies* 70(1) (2014) 1–7.

———. "Redressing the past, doing justice in the present: Necessary paradoxes." *HTS Teologiese Studies/Theological Studies* 75(4) (2019) a5625. https://doi.org/10.4102/hts.v75i4.5625

Van Wyk, I. W. C. "Calvin, Luther and Church Unity." *In die Skriflig* 44 (2010) 215–31.

Venter, Rian. "Space, Trinity and City: A theological exploration." *Acta Theologica* 26(1) (2006) 201–24.

———. "Speaking God today: The adventures of the rediscovered Trinitarian grammar." Inaugural lecture, University of the Free State. Bloemfontein: SUN Media, UFS, 2011.

Volf, Miroslav. *After our Likeness: The Church as the Image of the Trinity*. Grand Rapids, MI: Eerdmans, 1998.

———. *Exclusion and Embrace: a Theological Exploration of Identity, Otherness, and Reconciliation*. Nashville: Abingdon, 1996.

Vuntarde, Paul C. V. and Van Oort, Johannes. "Augustine's Ecclesiology and Its Development between 354 and 387 AD: Original Research." *HTS Theological Studies* 69(1) (2013) 1–5.

Wainwright, Geoffrey and Westerfield Tucker, Karen B. *The Oxford History of Christian Worship*. Oxford: Oxford University Press, 2006.

Wepener, Cas, and Barnard, Marcel. "Entering the Field: Initiating Liturgical Research in an AIC." *Acta Theologica* 30(2) (2010) 192–210.

Wepener, Cas. ""Bliksem!"/Damn it! A Ritual-Liturgical Appreciation of a Deadly Sin for an Angry Nation." *Verbum et Ecclesia* 36(3) (2015) Art. #1422, 8 pages. http://dx.doi.org/10.4102/ve.v36i3.1422.

———. *From Fast to Feast: a Ritual-Liturgical Exploration of Reconciliation in South African Cultural Contexts*. Dudley: Peeters, 2009.

———. "Gebed in die Liturgie: 'n Praktiese-Teologiese Verkenning." *Acta Theologica* 32(1) (2012) 189–209.

———. "Liturgical Inculturation or Liberation? A Qualitative Exploration of Major Themes in Liturgical Reform in South Africa." *HTS Theological Studies* 70(1) (2014) Art. #2644, 8 pages. http://dx.doi.org/10.4102/hts.v70i1.2644

———. "Liturgy on the Edge of Tradition." *Practical Theology in South Africa* 23(2) (2008) 313–35.

Bibliography

———. "The Object and Aim of Multi-Disciplinary Liturgical Research." *Scriptura: International Journal of Bible, Religion and Theology in Southern Africa* 93(1) (2006) 384–97.

———. "Participation and power. Opportunities for Method and Theory in Liturgical Research from a Changing (Dutch Reformed) South African Liturgical Landscape." *Nederduitse Gereformeerde Teologiese Tydskrif (NGTT)* 48(3&4) (2007) 730–42. http://ojs.reformedjournals.co.za/index.php/ngtt/article/view/392/755ß

———. "Reflections on Recent Developments in Liturgical Studies in the Light of Experiences from the Research Field and the Lecture Room." *Journal of Theology for South Africa* 144 (2012) 109–25.

———. "Researching Rituals: On the Use of Participatory Action Research in Liturgical Studies." *Practical Theology in South Africa* 20(1) (2005) 109–27.

———. "Ritual Route Markers for Reconciliation: Insights from a South African Exploration." *Theologia Viatorum* 36(2) (2012) 291–310.

———. *Van voor die Wieg tot na die Graf*. Wellington: Bybelkor, 2014.

Wigger, John. "American Methodist Worship. Karen B. Westerfield Tucker." *The Journal of Religion* 83(4) (2003) 621–22.

Willimon, William H. *Worship as Pastoral Care*. Nashville: Abingdon, 1979.

White, James F. *Introduction to Christian Worship*, 3rd edition, revised and expanded. Nashville: Abingdon, 2000.

Wolterstoff, Nicolas. *Justice in Love*. Grand Rapids, MI: Eerdmans, 2011.

Work, Telford. "Pentecostal and Charismatic worship." In *The Oxford History of Christian Worship*, edited by Geoffrey Wainwright and Karen B. Westerfield Tucker. Oxford: Oxford University Press, 2006.

Zizioulas, John and McPartlan, Paul, ed. *Communion and Otherness: Further Studies in Personhood and the Church*. London: T&T Clark, 2007.

Zizioulas, John D. *Being as Communion: Studies in Personhood and the Church*. Crestwood, NY: St Vladimir's Seminary Press, 1985.

———. *Communion and Otherness: Further Studies in Personhood and the Church*. London: T&T Clark, 2006.

www.ingramcontent.com/pod-product-compliance
Lightning Source LLC
Chambersburg PA
CBHW072133160426

43197CB00012B/2088